Continental's

Jump Start

Credits:

ILLUSTRATIONS: Front Cover: www.shutterstock.com, Matthew Cole; Denny Bond, Laurie Conley, Margaret Lindmark, Rob Williams, Jane Yamada

PHOTOS: Page 25: Chincoteague Chamber of Commerce, Chincoteague, Virginia; Page 49: *Mozart* Library of Congress, Prints and Photographs Division, LC-C420-2370; Page 53: www.photos.com; Page 55: US Fish and Wildlife Service; Page 104: *swimmer* www.photos.com; *runners* www.shutterstock.com, Morgan Lane Photography; Page 113: iStockphoto/Thinkstock; Page 132: www.istockphoto.com/wrangel; Page 136: Library of Congress, Prints and Photographs Division, LC-USZ-50927

ISBN 978-0-8454-7808-0

Copyright © 2014 The Continental Press, Inc.

Continental

D1211344

Table of Contents

Using *Continental's Jump Start*

Continental's Jump Start will help you prepare for the next level of your education. You have just finished grade 5 and will be entering grade 6 in the fall. *Continental's Jump Start* will help you review English language arts and math skills from grade 5. Then you will have a jump start on grade 6; the important ideas you learned last year will be fresh in your mind when the new school year starts.

This book is divided into nine weeks of review. Each day, you will do English language arts and math review. After four weeks, you will do the Midpoint Review. This will help you think about everything you worked on in the first four weeks. After you have completed the book, you will take the End-of-Book Review. You will have to remember the things you worked on in the last five weeks. There may be a few skills from the first four weeks in this review, too. When you have finished the entire book, you will receive a certificate to celebrate your hard work!

At the end of this book are some tools to help you. First, there is a glossary. The glossary has important words in it to help you with the English language arts pages. Check the glossary if you are not sure what a word means. Next, there is a page of math tools. Cut out these tools and use them whenever you need them for the math pages. Finally, there is an answer key. You can check your answers using the answer key.

The Midpoint Review and End-of-Book Review look like tests you take in school. They help you practice your test-taking skills. Some of the reading questions have two parts. For some of them you will have to write an answer. For math, you will do multiple-choice and open-ended items. Some of the multiple-choice items have more than one answer. Always read the questions carefully. You will be given 45 minutes for both the reading and the math portions of the reviews.

Each day, you will take about 30–45 minutes to complete the worksheets. The front of each worksheet covers English language arts skills and the back covers math concepts. There are two pages for the last day of each week. On this day, you will do a reading comprehension page with a passage and questions that go along with it. This page also includes a writing prompt that you will complete on a separate sheet of paper. You may need extra time to finish the pages on the fifth day.

Once you have completed this workbook, you will be ready to start a new grade in the fall. You will have practiced important English language arts and math skills, as well as your test-taking skills.

NOUNS

biography	horizon	divide	inspector
refuse	ingredient	diamond	boulder
melody	foggy	acre	construction
flatter	ringing	architect	ostrich
pilot	suffer	waken	translate
gigantic	assembly	telephone	silly

1. Frank Lloyd Wright was a famous _____.

2. A _____ is the hardest stone on Earth.

3. That's a catchy _____ you're humming.

4. The _____ does not really bury its head in the sand.

5. Most homes are built on less than one _____.

6. We have an _____ every Friday at school.

7. Our _____ checked with the tower before taking off.

8. The _____ is where the earth meets the sky.

9. The police _____ asked a lot of questions.

10. Have you read the new _____ of Barack Obama?

11. The most important _____ is the eggs.

12. The _____ fell from the mountaintop.

13. Please answer the _____!

14. The _____ on the highway caused us to be late.

MULTIPLYING WITH MULTIPLES OF TEN

Complete.

1. $(3 \times 7) \times 10 = \rule{2em}{0.4pt} \times \rule{2em}{0.4pt} = \rule{2em}{0.4pt}$

    $3 \times (7 \times 10) = \rule{2em}{0.4pt} \times \rule{2em}{0.4pt} = \rule{2em}{0.4pt}$

2. $(5 \times 9) \times 10 = \rule{2em}{0.4pt} \times \rule{2em}{0.4pt} = \rule{2em}{0.4pt}$

    $5 \times (9 \times 10) = \rule{2em}{0.4pt} \times \rule{2em}{0.4pt} = \rule{2em}{0.4pt}$

3. $(7 \times 6) \times 100 = \rule{2em}{0.4pt} \times \rule{2em}{0.4pt} = \rule{2em}{0.4pt}$

    $7 \times (6 \times 100) = \rule{2em}{0.4pt} \times \rule{2em}{0.4pt} = \rule{2em}{0.4pt}$

Multiply.

4. $\begin{array}{r} 60 \\ \times 1 \\ \hline \end{array}$	5. $\begin{array}{r} 60 \\ \times 2 \\ \hline \end{array}$	6. $\begin{array}{r} 60 \\ \times 3 \\ \hline \end{array}$	7. $\begin{array}{r} 60 \\ \times 4 \\ \hline \end{array}$	8. $\begin{array}{r} 60 \\ \times 5 \\ \hline \end{array}$
9. $\begin{array}{r} 40 \\ \times 9 \\ \hline \end{array}$	10. $\begin{array}{r} 30 \\ \times 8 \\ \hline \end{array}$	11. $\begin{array}{r} 50 \\ \times 3 \\ \hline \end{array}$	12. $\begin{array}{r} 20 \\ \times 6 \\ \hline \end{array}$	13. $\begin{array}{r} 80 \\ \times 5 \\ \hline \end{array}$
14. $\begin{array}{r} 300 \\ \times 1 \\ \hline \end{array}$	15. $\begin{array}{r} 300 \\ \times 2 \\ \hline \end{array}$	16. $\begin{array}{r} 300 \\ \times 3 \\ \hline \end{array}$	17. $\begin{array}{r} 300 \\ \times 4 \\ \hline \end{array}$	18. $\begin{array}{r} 300 \\ \times 5 \\ \hline \end{array}$
19. $\begin{array}{r} 200 \\ \times 4 \\ \hline \end{array}$	20. $\begin{array}{r} 600 \\ \times 6 \\ \hline \end{array}$	21. $\begin{array}{r} 500 \\ \times 7 \\ \hline \end{array}$	22. $\begin{array}{r} 700 \\ \times 8 \\ \hline \end{array}$	23. $\begin{array}{r} 400 \\ \times 9 \\ \hline \end{array}$

Find the answer to each word problem.

24. A car is traveling 65 miles per hour. A jet is traveling 10 times as fast. How fast is the jet traveling?

25. A theater showed a movie 4 times in one day. If 300 people saw the movie each time, how many people saw it that day?

POSSESSIVE FORM NOUNS

To make singular nouns show ownership, add an apostrophe and s ('s).

To make a plural noun that ends in s show ownership, add an apostrophe (').

To make a plural noun that does not end in s show ownership, add an apostrophe and s ('s).

Write the possessive form of the noun in parentheses to complete each sentence below.

1. Two of the race car _____ engines stalled.
   (drivers)

2. A lone _____ howl filled the night.
   (coyote)

3. The _____ glee club performed last night.
   (men)

4. _____ materials have gone way up in price.
   (Artists)

5. The _____ wool was extremely thick.
   (sheep)

6. The _____ helmets were lined up on the bench.
   (players)

7. The _____ performance was a critical success.
   (dancer)

8. The _____ instructions were helpful.
   (principal)

9. The _____ gifts are on the table.
   (children)

MULTIPLYING NUMBERS

Multiply. Regroup as often as you need to.

1. 24
   ×4

2. 47
   ×6

3. 51
   ×5

4. 15
   ×4

5. 26
   ×9

6. 72
   ×8

7. 176
   ×3

8. 244
   ×7

9. 703
   ×4

10. 324
    ×2

11. 243
    ×8

12. 399
    ×5

13. 427
    ×6

14. 296
    ×2

15. 832
    ×7

16. 961
    ×9

17. 9,315
    ×3

18. 5,187
    ×7

19. 7,682
    ×5

20. 2,593
    ×9

21. 8,078
    ×6

22. 10,046
    ×2

23. 21,600
    ×6

24. 18,418
    ×3

25. 97,285
    ×2

Multiply to find the total cost of each group of items below.

26. 3 orders of french fries at $0.65 each

27. 9 hot dogs at $1.19 each

28. 4 small lemonades at $0.57 each

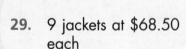

29. 9 jackets at $68.50 each

30. 6 suits at $257.38 each

31. 8 coats at $124.99 each

PRONOUN USAGE

These are **subject pronouns.**

    I   you   he   she   it   we   they

These are **object pronouns.**

    me   you   him   her   it   us   them

Circle the correct pronoun to complete each sentence.

The two of _____ sat quietly on the hill side. _____
            we   us   We   Us

were watching three brown bears. The largest was a female.

_____ was really huge. With _____ were two small cubs.
She   Her   she   her

It was July, and salmon were swimming upstream. The bears were

trying to catch _____. The cubs were not very successful.
              they   them

_____ jumped into the water many times, but the fish swam
They   Them

quickly away.

Then suddenly the bears began to run. _____ didn't know
                                 I   Me

what had scared _____. Then _____ saw _____.
               they   them   I   me   he   him

A 1200-pound male was lumbering toward the river! _____
                                          He   Him

was claiming this fishing spot. That was enough for _____.
                                          I   me

Like the mother and her cubs, _____ got out of there quickly.
                        we   us

TWO-DIGIT MULTIPLICATION

Multiply.

1.
$$\begin{array}{r} 45 \\ \times 32 \\ \hline \end{array}$$
← (2 × 45)
← (30 × 45)
← (_____ + _____)

2.
$$\begin{array}{r} 932 \\ \times 56 \\ \hline \end{array}$$
← (6 × 932)
← (50 × 932)
← (_____ + _____)

3.
$$\begin{array}{r} 55 \\ \times 26 \\ \hline \end{array}$$

4.
$$\begin{array}{r} 43 \\ \times 74 \\ \hline \end{array}$$

5.
$$\begin{array}{r} 38 \\ \times 85 \\ \hline \end{array}$$

6.
$$\begin{array}{r} 26 \\ \times 92 \\ \hline \end{array}$$

7.
$$\begin{array}{r} 216 \\ \times 42 \\ \hline \end{array}$$

8.
$$\begin{array}{r} 193 \\ \times 36 \\ \hline \end{array}$$

9.
$$\begin{array}{r} 232 \\ \times 61 \\ \hline \end{array}$$

10.
$$\begin{array}{r} 138 \\ \times 95 \\ \hline \end{array}$$

11.
$$\begin{array}{r} 57 \\ \times 16 \\ \hline \end{array}$$

12.
$$\begin{array}{r} 4,262 \\ \times 34 \\ \hline \end{array}$$

13.
$$\begin{array}{r} 5,073 \\ \times 56 \\ \hline \end{array}$$

14.
$$\begin{array}{r} 74 \\ \times 35 \\ \hline \end{array}$$

Find the answer to each word problem.

14. A shipment of 24 sweaters arrives at a store. The sweaters sell for $32 each. What is the total value of the shipment of sweaters?

14. A store gave away 25 gift cards at its grand opening. Each card was worth $150. What was the total value of the gift cards?

POSSESSIVE PRONOUNS

Possessive pronouns take the place of nouns that show ownership.

Joan's costume ⟶ her costume

Complete these sentences by writing a possessive pronoun to take the place of the possessive form noun or phrase in parentheses.

A giant pine cast _____ shadow on the lake. The moon
                    (the pine's)

was shining through _____ branches. Two friends stood
               (the pine's)

quiet on the shore. They kept _____ voices low.
                  (the friends')

"I don't hear _____ footsteps anymore," Kurt
           (the man's)

whispered to Pam. "It's time for _____ escape."
                (Kurt and Pam's)

Pam pushed _____ boat into the water with _____
       (Kurt and Pam's)   (Pam's)

foot. Kurt began to row with all _____ might.
                (Kurt's)

"Turn on _____ flashlight," said Pam to Kurt. "_____
       (Kurt's)   (Pam's)

map shows a ranger station around the next bend. Keep _____
                         (Kurt's)

eyes open. It may be _____ last chance."
             (Kurt and Pam's)

THREE-DIGIT MULTIPLICATION

Multiply.

1.
$$826 \times 174$$

2.
$$742 \times 209$$

3.
$$480 \times 683$$

4.
$$365 \times 715$$

5.
$$914 \times 521$$

6.
$$310 \times 936$$

7.
$$650 \times 705$$

8.
$$879 \times 243$$

9.
$$422 \times 198$$

10.
$$582 \times 847$$

11. It cost $7.50 to enter a cat in the cat show. If 213 cats were entered, how much money was collected on entry fees?

12. A ticket to the cat show cost $8.75. On the first day, 890 tickets were sold. How much money was collected on the tickets?

13. Valerie makes cat name tags. She sold 648 tags for $4.95 each. How much money did she take in?

14. Neal sold T-shirts at the cat show for $9.32 each. He sold 967 T-shirts in one day. How much money did Neal collect?

Read the passage. Then answer the questions.

Why Opossum Has a Pouch

a retelling of a Louisiana Koasati Tribe legend

1 One evening, a mama Opossum was in a field playing with her babies. Big Bat came swooping down and stole her little ones. Opossum shouted and begged Bat to bring back her babies. But Bat said he would not, and instead he took them into a deep hole in a rock and watched over them.

2 Opossum walked around the forest crying. Brave Wolf heard her cries and came to her.

3 "What is wrong, Opossum?" Wolf asked.

4 "Bat took my babies and will not give them back," she replied sadly.

5 "If you show me where they are, I will get them back for you," Wolf offered.

6 So Opossum showed Wolf the deep hole in the rock where Bat hid her babies. Wolf walked through the dark forest area and came back yelling. "Sorry, I cannot help you."

7 Opossum was crying even louder than before. Bold Rabbit came to her asking what was wrong. When Opossum told her story, Rabbit offered to go and get the babies from Bat.

8 Rabbit went to the same place Wolf did and came back out yelling. "Sorry, I cannot help you."

9 Opossum was sadder than ever. Neither Brave Wolf nor Bold Rabbit could help her get her babies back. So she walked around the forest crying louder than ever.

10 Highland-Terrapin, a kind of a turtle, came to her and asked her what was wrong.

11 "Big Bat has taken my babies from me, and he will not give them back. Brave Wolf tried to get them. Bold Rabbit tried to get them. But both of them failed. Can you help me?" Opossum cried.

12 "I will get them for you," Highland-Terrapin said. "Show me where they are."

13 Opossum took Highland-Terrapin to the deep hole in the rock where Bat watched over her babies. Highland-Terrapin walked into the darkness and started yelling. Bat had thrown hot ash down in the path in front of Highland-Terrapin, which burned his feet.

14 Even though Highland-Terrapin was in pain, he kept moving forward. He saw the baby opossums huddled together crying for their mother. Highland-Terrapin saw Big Bat above him, and he yelled at him for stealing the babies. Highland-Terrapin took the baby opossums out of the deep, dark hole and brought them back to their mother. The whole time, Big Bat was jumping on top of the terrapin's hard shell. Finally, Bat gave up and flew away.

15 When Highland-Terrapin returned with the babies, Opossum thanked him. Highland-Terrapin cut a hole in the belly of mama Opossum and put the babies inside. He told her, "Your babies have to stay in this belly pouch until they are old enough to eat on their own." From that day onward, mama opossums carry their babies in pouches near their bellies.

1. What is this story trying to explain?

   A   how bats try to steal opossum babies

   B   how terrapins are brave and strong

   C   how mama opossums carry babies

   D   how wolves and rabbits are weak

2. Which is the topic sentence of paragraph 14?

   A   "Even though Highland-Terrapin was in pain, he kept moving forward."

   B   "He saw the baby opossums huddled together crying for their mother."

   C   "Highland-Terrapin took the baby opossums out of the deep, dark hole and brought them back to their mother."

   D   "Finally, Bat gave up and flew away."

3. What was the mama opossum doing when Big Bat stole her babies?

   A   looking for food in a field

   B   looking for food in the forest

   C   playing in a field

   D   playing in the forest

4. Which of these is the best summary of the story?

   A   A terrapin steals Opossum's babies to teach her a lesson. Then she has a bat watch over them. When the terrapin returns the babies, he makes a pouch in Opossum for her babies.

   B   Opossum loses her babies in a field. A wolf, rabbit, and terrapin try to get them back. The terrapin makes a pouch in Opossum for her babies.

   C   A wolf, rabbit, and terrapin try to steal Opossum's babies. The bat looks after them. Opossum makes a pouch to carry her babies in.

   D   Bat takes Opossum's babies. A wolf, rabbit, and terrapin try to get the babies back. The terrapin is successful and makes a pouch for Opossum to keep her babies in.

5. Answer the following question on a separate piece of paper.

   Who was the strongest character in the story? Give two details that would support your opinion.

THREE-DIGIT MULTIPLICATION

1. 523×364

2. 384×265

3. 683×417

4. 472×516

5. 149×371

6. 207×628

7. 351×824

8. 628×715

9. 436×942

10. 186×275

11. 805×812

12. 349×733

Find the answer to each word problem.

13. A farmer has 370 acres of corn. He gets an average of 115 bushels of corn per acre. How many bushels should he expect to get in all?

14. There are 231 people on a plane, including passengers and crew. The average weight of a person is 152 pounds. What is the total weight of the people on the plane?

PROBLEM SOLVING: TWO- AND THREE-DIGIT MULTIPLICATION

Find the answer to each word problem.

1. A certain jet plane travels at 560 miles per hour. At that speed, how far will it travel in 12 hours?

2. There are 735 pages in Les's dictionary. If there is an average of 26 words on every page, how many words are in the dictionary?

3. LaVonda has 36 pictures on her digital camera. They have an average size of 160 kilobytes. How many kilobytes do the pictures take up altogether?

4. A medium-size serving of fries has 384 calories. If Mark orders medium fries 25 times a year, how many calories does he get from them?

5. A factory produces 44 miles of rope each week. There are 1,760 yards in a mile. How many yards of rope does the factory produce a week?

6. A football stadium has 124 rows of seats. If there are 248 seats in each row, how many seats are in the stadium?

7. A business bought 165 new computers. The computers cost $682 each. How much did they cost in all?

8. There are 236 rows of pepper plants in a field. Each row has 152 plants. How many pepper plants are in the field?

s-FORM VERBS

Use the plain form of a verb with a plural subject.
Use the s-form with a singular subject.

Make the s-form of most verbs by
adding -s.

> defeat ——→ defeats

Make the s-form of verbs that end in x,
s, ch, or sh by adding -es.

> crouch ——→ crouches

Make the s-form of verbs that end in a
consonant plus y by changing the y to i
and adding -es.

> apply ——→ applies

Write the s-form of each verb below.

1. volunteer

_____

2. sketch

_____

3. watch

_____

4. exist

_____

5. envy

_____

6. identify

_____

7. relax

_____

8. flatter

_____

9. mash

_____

10. magnify

_____

11. supply

_____

12. publish

_____

13. establish

_____

14. intend

_____

ONE-DIGIT DIVISION

1. $4\overline{)120}$ 2. $3\overline{)240}$ 3. $5\overline{)155}$ 4. $2\overline{)148}$

5. $9\overline{)414}$ 6. $6\overline{)192}$ 7. $8\overline{)184}$ 8. $5\overline{)310}$

9. $5\overline{)482}$ 10. $2\overline{)132}$ 11. $8\overline{)352}$ 12. $9\overline{)265}$

13. $2\overline{)184}$ 14. $8\overline{)369}$ 15. $5\overline{)160}$ 16. $7\overline{)133}$

Find the answer to each word problem.

17. There are 147 people at a tree-planting event. They break into groups of 3 people to plant trees. How many groups are formed?

18. Ms. Harris has 480 insurance forms to process. She can process 9 forms an hour. How many hours will it take to process all the forms?

PAST VERB FORMS

Write the past form of each verb in parentheses to complete the sentences below. Use a dictionary if you need help.

James Marshall _____ his house early one winter
(leave)

morning in 1848. He _____ to the nearby river to
(go)

begin work for the day. As Marshall looked into the water, he

_____ something shine. He _____ the shiny
(see)   (take)

object in his hand and hurried over to some other workers.

"Boys," Marshall _____, "I believe I _____
(say)   (find)

a gold mine!"

In fact, he _____. Marshall and his friends
(have)

_____ they could keep the gold a secret. But
(think)

people _____ about it. The news _____
(tell)   (get)

around. Soon newspaper reporters _____ about it.
(write)

Gold fever _____ rapidly. People _____ to
(grow)   (come)

California from all over the world. Some of them _____
(make)

their fortunes. But most 49ers _____ not get rich.
(do)

DIVIDING BY TWO-DIGIT NUMBERS

Divide. Check by multiplying. Remember to add any remainder.

1. $42 \overline{)950}$

2. $18 \overline{)414}$

3. $29 \overline{)900}$

4. $57 \overline{)741}$

5. $63 \overline{)2,840}$

6. $84 \overline{)2,352}$

7. $92 \overline{)6,495}$

8. $27 \overline{)1,809}$

9. $52 \overline{)3,908}$

10. $65 \overline{)2,549}$

11. $39 \overline{)3,471}$

12. $91 \overline{)1,638}$

13. $3,087 \div 63 =$ _____

14. $8,460 \div 96 =$ _____

15. Uptown Bakery made 5,976 cookies today. If 72 cookies were put in a bag, how many bags were filled?

16. Lynette can make 1,128 doughnuts from a batch of dough. She can pack 12 doughnuts in a box. How many boxes can Lynette fill with a batch of dough?

IRREGULAR VERB FORMS

Write the correct verb forms to complete these sentences.

Ms. Dahl has _____ to our class about the monarch
spoke   spoken

butterfly. She has _____ articles about it for famous
wrote   written

magazines. Her search for the monarch _____ her to many
took   taken

countries. To track this insect, she has _____ jeeps and has
drove   driven

_____ mules.
rode   ridden

One mystery was where the monarchs _____ for the
flew   flown

winter. Until 1975, no one _____. Finally Ms. Dahl discovered
knew   known

that they _____ to the mountains of Mexico. The monarchs
went   gone

stay there until new butterflies have _____. By spring,
grew   grown

another journey north will have _____.
began   begun

Ms. Dahl showed us pictures of the area. In one, scattered wings

showed that birds have _____ whole flocks of monarchs.
ate   eaten

We also _____ great masses of butterflies, as though a
saw   seen

breeze had _____ them into a cloud. In one photo, the
blew   blown

monarchs completely _____ a tree.
hid   hidden

DIVIDING BY TWO-DIGIT NUMBERS

Divide. Check by multiplying. Remember to add any remainder.

1. $32\overline{)4,504}$

2. $41\overline{)9,677}$

3. $53\overline{)5,671}$

4. $69\overline{)10,490}$

5. $28\overline{)18,063}$

6. $75\overline{)72,225}$

7. $15,436 \div 17 =$ _____

8. $22,724 \div 92 =$ _____

9. $33,060 \div 58 =$ _____

10. $11,772 \div 54 =$ _____

ADJECTIVES

Adjectives tell something about nouns. An adjective usually comes before the noun it tells about.

A <u>wild</u> bear is a <u>fierce</u> animal.

Rewrite each sentence.
Put one of the adjectives in parentheses before each underlined noun.

1. This <u>bread</u> has a <u>taste</u>.   (fresh, good)

   _____

2. The <u>horses</u> had <u>legs</u>.   (young, thin)

   _____

3. The <u>basket</u> was full of <u>fruit</u>.   (heavy, fresh)

   _____

4. This <u>pencil</u> needs a <u>point</u>.   (small, sharp)

   _____

5. The <u>boy</u> drew a <u>picture</u>.   (creative, comical)

   _____

6. The <u>group</u> climbed the <u>mountain</u>.   (large, tall)

   _____

7. The <u>necklace</u> is made of <u>beads</u>.   (pretty, glass)

   _____

DIVISION WITH MULTIPLES OF TEN

Divide.

1. $360 \div 90 =$ _____
   $3,600 \div 90 =$ _____
   $36,000 \div 90 =$ _____

2. $240 \div 30 =$ _____
   $2,400 \div 30 =$ _____
   $24,000 \div 30 =$ _____

3. $420 \div 70 =$ _____
   $4,200 \div 70 =$ _____
   $42,000 \div 70 =$ _____

4. $24 \div 4 =$ _____
   $240 \div 4 =$ _____
   $2,400 \div 4 =$ _____

5. $49 \div 7 =$ _____
   $490 \div 7 =$ _____
   $4,900 \div 7 =$ _____

6. $30 \div 5 =$ _____
   $300 \div 5 =$ _____
   $3,000 \div 5 =$ _____

7. $560 \div 80 =$ _____
   $5,600 \div 80 =$ _____
   $56,000 \div 80 =$ _____

8. $48 \div 8 =$ _____
   $480 \div 8 =$ _____
   $4,800 \div 8 =$ _____

9. $400 \div 80 =$ _____
   $4,000 \div 80 =$ _____
   $40,000 \div 80 =$ _____

10. $70\overline{)490}$

11. $60\overline{)180}$

12. $80\overline{)320}$

13. $90\overline{)720}$

14. $30\overline{)1,200}$

15. $80\overline{)2,400}$

16. $50\overline{)2,500}$

17. $40\overline{)1,600}$

18. $6\overline{)180}$

19. $7\overline{)280}$

20. $8\overline{)320}$

21. $9\overline{)630}$

22. $3\overline{)1,500}$

23. $8\overline{)2,400}$

24. $5\overline{)4,500}$

25. $4\overline{)1,200}$

COMPREHENSION: CAUSE AND EFFECT

Read the passage. Then answer the questions.

Chincoteague's Pony Swim

1   On Assateague Island, off the coast of Virginia, something strange happens every year. Each year since 1925, about 100 ponies run wild late in July. By then, the ponies born that spring are big enough to be on their own. Volunteer firefighters from nearby Chincoteague Island herd them into a giant pen. The next day, the firefighters drive them into the water. The day is specially chosen so that the tides are just right for a swim. The ponies swim to Chincoteague, which is about a quarter of a mile away. The pony that makes it to shore first is crowned King or Queen Neptune and given away at the volunteer firefighters' carnival. The other ponies are sold at auction. Prices might go anywhere from $1,000 to $4,000. The new owners then take their ponies home. Those that aren't sold are herded back to Assateague Island. There, they run free for another year.

2   How did this annual event come about? If some of the ponies weren't sold, there would be too many on the island. Then

there wouldn't be enough food for them and the new foals born each spring. Eventually, some ponies would starve to death. Holding a pony auction each year is a way of making sure that Assateague Island doesn't have too many ponies. It's also a way for the volunteer firefighters to make money for Chincoteague's fire department. Thousands of people visit the town each year for the pony auction and carnival.

1.   **Part A**

What might happen to the ponies on Assateague Island if they were not sold?

A   They might starve to death.

B   They might stop having foals.

C   They might drown.

D   They might attack people.

Part B

Underline the sentence in the passage that helped you find your answer to Part A.

2. What is the main reason the pony swim is held in late July?

   A so that people can go to the carnival

   B because that is when the tide is right for the swim

   C because that is the time people chose in 1925

   D because there are too many ponies at this time of year

3. What happens to the ponies that are not sold on Chincoteague Island?

   A They run free on Chincoteague Island.

   B They run free on Assateague Island.

   C They are taken to other islands for sale.

   D They stay in a giant pen until the spring.

4. One pony is the first to reach shore each year. Which of the following is not an effect of being the first pony to reach shore?

   A It is given away at the carnival.

   B It no longer lives on Assateague.

   C It is crowned King or Queen Neptune.

   D It is herded back to Assateague.

5. Answer the following question on a separate piece of paper.

   Why do the volunteer firefighters hold the pony auction? Use details from the passage to support your answer.

TWO-DIGIT DIVISION

Divide. Check using multiplication.

1. $46\overline{)1,384}$

2. $27\overline{)733}$

3. $94\overline{)1,130}$

4. $53\overline{)1,643}$

5. $81\overline{)42,303}$

6. $48\overline{)2,088}$

7. $19\overline{)990}$

8. $72\overline{)22,875}$

9. $78\overline{)4,758}$

10. $46\overline{)1,610}$

11. $14\overline{)5,120}$

12. $39\overline{)3,978}$

Find the answer to each word problem.

13. Joann packs 28 grapefruits into each sack for sale. If Joann had 427 grapefruits, how many sacks can she fill?

14. A mile is 5,280 feet. A swimming pool is 75 feet long. How many times must Ethan swim the length of the pool to swim a mile?

PROBLEM SOLVING: TWO-DIGIT DIVISION

Find the answer to each word problem.

1. Jasmine wants 450 cookies for her club's party. If 30 members bring cookies, how many cookies should each one bring?

2. The battery in a radio is guaranteed for 600 hours. How many days will it last if the radio is played 24 hours a day?

3. Dee drives an average of 85 kilometers per hour. At that rate, how long will it take her to drive 2,040 kilometers?

4. Joelle earned $1,012 last month at her part-time job. She worked 22 days. How much did she earn each day?

5. Malik's book has 675 pages. If he reads 54 pages every day, how many days will it take him to read his book?

6. Mr. Mehta puts 25 potatoes in each bag. How many bags will he need for 980 potatoes? How many potatoes will he have left over?

7. George wants to buy a kayak that costs $1,600. He can save $75 a month. At that rate, how many months will it take him to save enough for the kayak?

8. Workers are setting up chairs in a gym. If they have 1,690 chairs, how many rows of 48 chairs can they make? How many chairs will be left?

COMPARING WITH ADJECTIVES

Add -er or -r to most adjectives to compare two things.

thicker   purer

Add -est or -st to most adjectives to compare three or more things.

thickest   purest

For some adjectives, double the final consonant before adding -er or -est.

For adjectives that end in a consonant plus y, change the y to i before adding -er or -est.

For adjectives with many syllables, use more or most instead of an ending.

Write the forms that compare for each adjective below.

		TO COMPARE TWO	TO COMPARE THREE OR MORE
1.	slim		
2.	valuable		
3.	dim		
4.	risky		
5.	honest		
6.	wide		
7.	polite		
8.	warm		
9.	big		
10.	silly		
11.	sad		
12.	tasty		
13.	pleasant		

PLACE VALUE: LARGE NUMBERS

Write each number in standard form.

1. $10,000 + 6,000 + 400 + 50 + 7 =$ _____

2. $30,000 + 4,000 + 100 + 60 + 5 =$ _____

3. $70,000 + 900 + 10 + 3 =$ _____

4. $10,000 + 8,000 + 500 =$ _____

5. $900,000 + 50,000 + 1,000 + 900 + 80 + 7 =$ _____

6. $400,000 + 6,000 + 90 =$ _____

7. eighty thousand, five hundred twenty-three = _____

8. thirty-two thousand, one hundred sixty-two = _____

9. seventeen thousand, forty = _____

10. five hundred nineteen thousand, six hundred fifteen = _____

11. four hundred thousand, two hundred twelve = _____

Write each number in expanded form.

12. $27,916 =$ _____

13. $85,875 =$ _____

14. $72,000 =$ _____

15. $394,000 =$ _____

16. $510,081 =$ _____

17. $193,567 =$ _____

Write the total value of the underlined digit.

18. $7\underline{6},054 =$ _____

19. $\underline{5}1,625 =$ _____

20. $78,0\underline{3}0 =$ _____

21. $25,0\underline{1}9 =$ _____

22. $\underline{9}2,615 =$ _____

23. $12\underline{4},165 =$ _____

24. $8\underline{0}5,127 =$ _____

25. $3\underline{6}0,100 =$ _____

26. $174,9\underline{1}4 =$ _____

27. $201,3\underline{9}8 =$ _____

ADVERBS

Adverbs tell how, when, or where things are done.

yesterday	again	here	tomorrow
away	always	already	well

Circle the adverb in each sentence.

1. You can park your car here in the driveway.

2. Our neighbors moved away to a different state.

3. Dad will fix the roof tomorrow.

4. The basketball team played well.

5. We went swimming yesterday at the pool.

6. Luisa already invited her friends to the picnic.

7. The light on the smoke detector flashed again.

8. Ahmed always complains about the cafeteria food.

9. We had pizza and salad for lunch today.

10. She knocked at the door, but no one was there.

ROUNDING LARGE NUMBERS

Round each number to the nearest ten. Look at the ones digit. If it is 5 or more, round up. If it is 4 or less, round down.

1. 74 _____
2. 45 _____
3. 32 _____
4. 29 _____

5. 361 _____
6. 925 _____
7. 407 _____
8. 893 _____

9. 2,016 _____
10. 5,204 _____
11. 1,992 _____
12. 7,099 _____

Round each number to the nearest hundred. Look at the tens digit.

13. 155 _____
14. 429 _____
15. 316 _____
16. 292 _____

17. 541 _____
18. 763 _____
19. 1,450 _____
20. 4,893 _____

21. 3,216 _____
22. 2,684 _____
23. 8,090 _____
24. 6,999 _____

Round each number to the nearest thousand. Look at the hundreds digit.

25. 2,405 _____
26. 1,629 _____
27. 8,362 _____

28. 4,911 _____
29. 7,387 _____
30. 19,499 _____

31. 23,541 _____
32. 105,813 _____
33. 586,200 _____

Find the answer to each word problem.

34. The population of Middletown is 7,843. What is the population to the nearest hundred?

_____

What is the population to the nearest thousand?

_____

35. There are 2,456 cars in Middletown. What is this number to the nearest hundred?

_____

What is this number to the nearest thousand?

_____

USING ADJECTIVES AND ADVERBS

Adjectives tell about nouns or pronouns.
A hammer is a useful tool.
Adverbs tell about verbs, adjectives, or other adverbs.
Alicia waited patiently.

Above the underlined word in each sentence below, write adj. if it is an adjective or adv. if it is an adverb.

1. Brooke wears stylish clothes.

2. Peter likes food that is grown organically.

3. Ariel began a scientific experiment.

4. The blueberries were plentiful this year.

5. Sheila carelessly lost her keys.

6. Fold the egg whites into the mixture gently.

7. The nimble runner broke all the records.

8. Mrs. Duong will leave the hospital tomorrow.

9. We should put the chicken and ribs on separate plates.

10. I did really well on the test.

11. You need to see a dentist regularly.

12. Is that store vacant?

13. Do you still have the original email?

14. The talented singer had several encores.

COMPARING AND ORDERING NUMBERS

1. 56 ◯ 65

2. 2,109 ◯ 2,108

3. 49,798 ◯ 49,806

4. 734 ◯ 729

5. 4,284 ◯ 4,264

6. 32,495 ◯ 214,210

7. 409 ◯ 490

8. 9,884 ◯ 9,798

9. 950,301 ◯ 950,288

10. 8,706 ◯ 8,670

11. 10,370 ◯ 1,470

12. 814,000 ◯ 804,956

Below is a table showing the highest mountain on each continent. Write number sentences to compare the heights of the mountains for each pair of continents.

Continent	Mountain	Height in Feet
Africa	Kilimanjaro	19,340
Antarctica	Vinson	16,066
Asia	Everest	29,035
Australia	Kosciusko	7,310
Europe	Elbrus	18,510
North America	McKinley	20,320
South America	Aconcagua	22,834

13. Asia/South America

_____ ◯ _____

14. Australia/Antarctica

_____ ◯ _____

15. Europe/Africa

_____ ◯ _____

16. South America/North America

_____ ◯ _____

List the names of the mountains in order from highest to lowest.

_____

_____

_____

_____

_____

_____

COMPOUND WORDS

gold	shield	1.	_____
wind	port	2.	_____
air	house	3.	_____
drug	quarters	4.	_____
some	fish	5.	_____
light	shore	6.	_____
head	road	7.	_____
sea	store	8.	_____
rail	how	9.	_____

Sometimes a compound word is written as one word, sometimes as separate words, and sometimes with a hyphen connecting the small words.

eyebrow   high school   tongue-tied

Circle the compound word in each sentence below. Then write its separate parts on the line in front of the sentence.

_____ 10. The clowns put on their make-up and took their places.

_____ 11. During the art festival, the sidewalk was filled with people.

_____ 12. Hank Aaron hit 755 home runs during his long career.

_____ 13. My brother is the only left-handed person in our family.

_____ 14. Every Saturday, Carol baby-sits for her little cousin.

_____ 15. Terri screeched when she hit her funny bone on the desk.

_____ 16. The framework of the building looked like a giant steel web.

_____ 17. Huge waves smashed the beach at high tide.

_____ 18. Playing in the sunshine helps people stay healthy.

_____ 19. Last year, earthquakes hit the southern part of the state.

_____ 20. At camp, we slept in a cabin with bunk beds.

PRIME AND COMPOSITE NUMBERS

A **prime number** has exactly two factors, 1 and itself. For example, 7 is a prime number. Its only factors are 1 and 7.

A **composite number** has more than two factors. For example, 12 is a composite number. Its factors are 1, 2, 3, 4, 6, and 12.

Find all the factors of each number below. Then write <u>prime</u> or <u>composite</u> to describe it.

1. 4: _____

2. 5: _____

3. 6: _____

4. 8: _____

5. 10: _____

6. 11: _____

7. 13: _____

8. 15: _____

A composite number can be shown as the product of prime numbers using a **factor tree.** These factor trees show the **prime factorization** of 12. Notice that the bottom lines are the same.

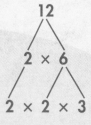
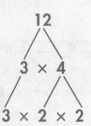

12
2 × 6
2 × 2 × 3

12
3 × 4
3 × 2 × 2

Complete each factor tree.

9.
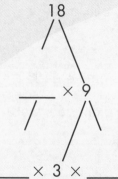
18
___ × 9
___ × 3 × ___

10.
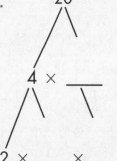
20
4 × ___
2 × ___ × ___

11.
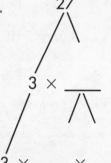
27
3 × ___
3 × ___ × ___

12.
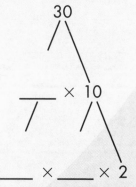
30
___ × 10
___ × ___ × 2

COMPREHENSION: ANALYZING LANGUAGE

Silver

by Walter de la Mare

Slowly, silently, now the moon
Walks the night in her silver shoon;
This way, and that, she peers, and sees
Silver fruit upon silver trees;
5 One by one the casements catch
Her beams beneath the silvery thatch;
Couched in his kennel, like a log,
With paws of silver sleeps the dog;
From their shadowy cote the white breasts peep
10 Of doves in a silver-feathered sleep;
A harvest mouse goes scampering by,
With silver claws, and silver eye;
And moveless fish in the water gleam,
By silver reeds in a silver stream.

1. Which two literary devices are used in lines 1 and 2?

   A simile and irony

   B personification and alliteration

   C hyperbole and idiom

   D understatement and irony

2. Which of these things in the poem is compared to a person?

   A the kennel

   B the fruit

   C the water

   D the moon

3. **Part A**

   The poet compares a sleeping dog to which of the following?

   A    C

   B    D

   Part B

   Underline the line or lines in the poem that best support your answer to Part A.

4. Explain why the poet sees everything cast with a silver tone.

   _____

   _____

5. Answer the following question on a separate piece of paper.
   Why does the poet repeat the word "silver" throughout the poem?

FACTORS

Factors are the numbers that are multiplied to get a product.
Find the multiplication facts for each number. Then list the factors in order.

	Facts	Factors
1. 12		
2. 5		
3. 6		
4. 8		
5. 10		
6. 15		
7. 18		
8. 20		
9. 24		
10. 30		
11. 32		
12. 36		
13. 40		
14. 45		
15. 48		
16. 54		

Find the common factors of each set of numbers. Circle the greatest common factor.

17. 5 and 10	22. 30 and 45
18. 10 and 15	23. 36 and 48
19. 6 and 12	24. 24 and 32
20. 8 and 24	25. 18 and 36
21. 15 and 40	26. 48 and 54

MULTIPLES

Multiples are the products of a factor and consecutive whole numbers.
List the first ten multiples of each number.

1. 3 _____
2. 2 _____
3. 4 _____
4. 5 _____
5. 6 _____
6. 7 _____
7. 8 _____
8. 9 _____
9. 10 _____
10. 12 _____
11. 15 _____
12. 20 _____
13. 30 _____
14. 50 _____
15. 100 _____
16. 1,000 _____

Find the common multiples of each set of numbers. Use the numbers above. Circle the least common multiple.

17. 3 and 12 _____
18. 3 and 5 _____
19. 2 and 10 _____
20. 4 and 5 _____
21. 4 and 6 _____

22. 4 and 8 _____
23. 6 and 9 _____
24. 10 and 15 _____
25. 12 and 15 _____
26. 50 and 100 _____

CAPITALIZATION

Rewrite the sentences below using correct capitalization.

1. i just read a book called <u>the living white house</u>.

   _____

   _____

2. it tells about people who have lived in the white house in washington, dc.

   _____

   _____

3. president harrison's grandson lived there with a pet goat named his whiskers.

   _____

   _____

4. tad lincoln kept a pet turkey that someone had sent his family for christmas dinner.

   _____

   _____

5. the book also tells about the egg-roll that is held on easter monday at the white house.

   _____

   _____

6. theodore roosevelt's children had a pony named fidelity.

   _____

   _____

7. tricia nixon was married in the rose garden at the white house.

   _____

   _____

DECIMALS: PLACE VALUE

Tenths, hundredths, and thousandths can be written as fractions or as decimals.

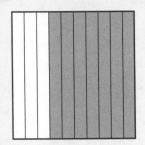

$\frac{7}{10} = 0.7$

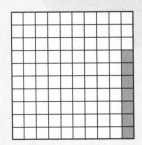

$\frac{7}{100} = 0.07$

$\frac{7}{1000} = 0.007$

Write each fraction or mixed number as a decimal.

1. $\frac{3}{10} =$ _____

2. $\frac{29}{100} =$ _____

3. $9\frac{102}{1000} =$ _____

4. $7\frac{45}{100} =$ _____

5. $\frac{74}{1000} =$ _____

6. $35\frac{9}{100} =$ _____

7. $\frac{38}{100} =$ _____

8. $\frac{982}{1000} =$ _____

9. $28\frac{8}{1000} =$ _____

10. $4\frac{99}{100} =$ _____

11. $\frac{406}{1000} =$ _____

12. $100\frac{1}{10} =$ _____

Write a decimal for each number name.

13. 8 and 2 tenths _____

14. 5 tenths _____

15. 1 and 73 hundredths _____

16. 26 hundredths _____

17. 2 and 205 thousandths _____

18. 47 and 6 thousandths _____

19. 17 hundredths _____

20. 8 and 52 thousandths _____

21. 400 and 2 tenths _____

22. 621 thousandths _____

23. 19 and 4 hundredths _____

24. 180 and 123 thousandths _____

FORMING SENTENCES

Write a noun from the box to complete each sentence.

Spiders	Students	Kites	Monkeys
Wounds	Lights	Mice	Steaks

1. _____ study.

2. _____ heal.

3. _____ climb.

4. _____ flicker.

5. _____ soar.

6. _____ scurry.

7. _____ spin.

8. _____ sizzle.

Write a verb from the box to complete each sentence.

burst	squeal	rattle	screech
block	whistle	blare	crumble

9. Windows _____.

10. Balloons _____.

11. Pigs _____.

12. Trains _____.

13. Brakes _____.

14. Horns _____

15. Goalies _____.

16. Cookies _____

COMPARING DECIMALS

Compare. Write >, <, or =.

1. 1.6 ◯ 1.06
2. 0.5 ◯ 0.8
3. 0.3 ◯ 0.2

4. 0.4 ◯ 4.0
5. 0.7 ◯ 0.70
6. 0.9 ◯ 0.09

7. 2.3 ◯ 3.2
8. 2.9 ◯ 2.8
9. 1.8 ◯ 8.1

10. 0.17 ◯ 0.19
11. 0.65 ◯ 0.36
12. 5.20 ◯ 0.52

13. 1.53 ◯ 1.45
14. 4.50 ◯ 4.05
15. 2.9 ◯ 2.90

16. 3.09 ◯ 3.90
17. 6.01 ◯ 6.1
18. 1.76 ◯ 0.79

Write each set of decimals in order from least to greatest.

19. 0.4, 0.3, 0.9 _____

20. 0.32, 0.05, 1.01 _____

21. 2.03, 3.4, 1.96 _____

Write each set of decimals in order from greatest to least.

22. 0.1, 0.6, 0.5 _____

23. 0.29, 0.92, 0.2 _____

24. 0.56, 4.09, 1.78 _____

Write a number sentence to find the answer to each word problem.

25. Linda mixes 0.2 kilogram of peanuts with 0.09 kilogram of raisins. Which does she use more of?

26. Urban walks 2.3 kilometers to school. He walks 2.15 kilometers to the library. Which distance is shorter?

SUBJECT AND PREDICATE

The **subject** of a sentence tells whom or what the sentence is about. The complete subject may include more than one word.

The **predicate** of a sentence tells what the subject is or was or does or did. The complete predicate may include more than one word.

A tiny tugboat rescued the huge ship.
complete subject   complete predicate

Underline once the complete subject of each sentence below.
Underline the complete predicate twice.

Bicycles were invented in the late 1700s. Two-wheelers came in many shapes and sizes for the next 90 years.

The first bicycle was called a *walk-along*. The walk-along had no pedals. The rider sat on it and pushed it with his or her feet.

The *boneshaker* appeared in the 1860s. Its wooden wheels gave riders a bumpy trip. The front wheel of this bicycle was slightly larger than the back wheel.

The *high wheeler* was one of the strangest bikes of all. Its front wheel measured 40–48 inches high. The back wheel was very small, however.

These early bicycles were funny to look at. They were also very hard to ride.

ADDING DECIMALS

1. 16.75
    + 9.25

2. 0.58
    +0.14

3. 0.043
    +0.267

4. 8.6
    +3.9

5. 15.76
    +42.96

6. 109.1
    +199.7

7. 3.857
    +5.806

8. 62.78
    +15.04

9. 498.75
    +487.59

10. 562.16
    +108.63

11. 25.834
    +60.179

12. 37.095
    +19.963

13. 10.84
    32.56
    + 4.92

14. 376.8
    109.4
    +253.4

15. 8.042
    4.731
    +1.659

16. 61.504
    30.298
    +27.153

Solve. Remember to line up the decimal points.

17. Dr. Wong is working 0.783 kilometer north of the ship. Dr. Kamal is 0.898 kilometer directly south of the ship. How far apart are they?

18. Mud sample A is a tube 20.8 centimeters long. Mud sample B is 11.7 centimeters longer than A. How long is sample B?

19. Dr. Wong collected 13.72 kilograms of rocks on her first dive and 19.89 kilograms on the second dive. How much do her samples weigh in all?

20. The current at Cape Nom travels 3.55 kilometers an hour. At Zen Point, it moves 4.77 kilometers an hour faster. How fast does it move there?

END PUNCTUATION

Write S before each statement, Q before each question, E before each exclamation, and C before each command. Put the correct punctuation mark at the end of each sentence.

_____ 1. We are exploring a cave

_____ 2. Never go into a cave alone

_____ 3. Proper equipment is important

_____ 4. Did you choose a leader

_____ 5. How experienced he is

_____ 6. He makes sure everyone is safe

_____ 7. What a difficult job he has

_____ 8. Are you dressed warmly

_____ 9. Be sure to have your supplies

_____ 10. Is the cave up ahead

_____ 11. Go in through this entrance

_____ 12. What an exciting trip this will be

SUBTRACTING DECIMALS

Subtract.

1. 12.98
    − 9.75

2. 9.6
    −4.9

3. 0.74
    −0.28

4. 0.243
    −0.065

5. 409.1
    −299.7

6. 8.306
    −6.357

7. 52.76
    −13.86

8. 6.140
    −3.942

9. 308.75
    −209.77

10. 70.153
    −69.294

11. 25.934
    − 8.976

12. 94.504
    −30.928

13. 4.052
    −2.386

14. 376.80
    −176.81

15. 60.01
    −40.32

16. 86.200
    − 6.345

Solve. Remember to line up the decimal points.

17. One trail to Gold Creek is 9.75 miles long. Another trail is 14.81 miles long. How much longer is the second trail than the first?

18. Kirsten's pack weighs 21.8 pounds. Graham's pack weighs 24.3 pounds. How much heavier is Graham's pack?

19. During the day, the temperature rose to 78.8°F. At night, it fell to 45.9°F. How many degrees did the temperature drop?

20. Kirsten found 0.013 ounce of gold in the creek. Graham found 0.006 ounce. How much more gold did Kirsten find than Graham?

Beethoven and Mozart

by Frederick Smith

1   Wolfgang Amadeus Mozart and Ludwig van Beethoven may have both spoken German, but they were not both from Germany. Mozart was actually from Austria, and he was born 14 years before Beethoven was. Beethoven did move to Austria early in his life. So, eventually, both men composed music in Austria. Both of these men became well known for playing the piano. But it was their writing of music, or composing, that led them to fame.

2   But Beethoven has another claim to fame that you may or may not know about: Later in his life, he lost his hearing. Somehow, he was still able to compose great musical pieces. People were amazed that he could write the music without being able to hear it.

3   Although Mozart did not lose his hearing, he did overcome much in his life as well. His father taught him how to play piano at a very young age. Then his father took Mozart traveling to play for royalty all over Europe. Mozart was only 6 years old! Often he was hired as a court musician to support his family. Sometimes he was treated like a musical slave. This caused him a lot of stress.

Mozart

4   While Mozart and Beethoven both wrote music as they were going through personal struggles, they wrote in very different musical styles. Many people would call both of them "classical" composers, but this term is really too general. In the early days of Beethoven's composing, many people thought his music sounded a bit like Mozart's. But as time went on, their music started to sound more different. Beethoven wanted his music to sound different.

Beethoven

While Mozart wrote his music using the same format that most composers had used, Beethoven tried to write music that did not follow the rules. Although you probably think of classical music as being pretty tame, Beethoven was more of a rebel when it came to his music.

5   Beethoven and Mozart have something in common besides music: They both fell in love with women who did not return their feelings. Beethoven wrote a famous love letter, most likely to a woman named Antonia Brentano. This woman did not return his love, and so Beethoven never married in his life. Mozart also confessed his love to a woman who did not feel the same way: Mozart fell in love with a woman named Aloysia Weber. When she said that she did not feel the same way, Mozart married her sister.

6   The next time someone asks you if you like classical music, remember that not all classical music is the same. While Beethoven's music sounds like Mozart's in many ways, Beethoven worked to break the rules. Both men overcame troubles in their lives, although their individual experiences were each very different.

1. Which of these best describes how the article organizes information?

   A   It first talks about Beethoven and then about Mozart.

   B   It first talks about Mozart and then about Beethoven.

   C   It first contrasts the musicians and then compares them.

   D   It compares and contrasts both musicians point by point.

2. **Part A**

   According to the author, what is the main difference between Mozart's and Beethoven's music at the time they wrote it?

   _____

   _____

   Part B

   Underline the sentence that helped you find your answer to Part A.

3. Which of the following is true for both Beethoven and Mozart?

   A   They traveled as a child piano player.

   B   They had their hearts broken.

   C   They broke rules with music.

   D   They went deaf late in life.

4. Which of these shows a way that Beethoven and Mozart were different?

   A   Mozart was born in Austria.

   B   Beethoven lived in Austria.

   C   Mozart is a classical composer.

   D   Beethoven overcame a struggle.

5. Answer the following question on a separate piece of paper.

   Think of your favorite rock star, rapper, or singer. Compare and contrast that person to either Mozart or Beethoven.

ADDING AND SUBTRACTING DECIMALS

Rewrite each problem in vertical form. Write in zeros to help you. Then solve.

1. 52.6 + 18.43 =

2. 63.51 − 14.7 =

3. 8.472 + 0.9 =

4. 92.3 − 82.64 =

5. 405 − 27.9 =

6. 73.4 + 629 =

7. 16.01 + 8.592 =

8. 32.4 − 29.685 =

9. 8.4 + 25.76 =

10. 32.09 − 14.8 =

11. 65.12 − 8.234 =

12. 29.7 + 6.85 + 3.6 =

Solve. Remember to line up the decimal points.

13. Cassandra has 3 meters of canvas. If she uses 1.25 meters of it to stretch over a frame for a painting, how much will be left?

14. Chad's sculpture weighs 23.5 kilograms. He welds a piece that weighs 3.74 kilograms onto it. How much does it weigh now?

PROBLEM SOLVING: ADDING AND SUBTRACTING DECIMALS

Read and solve each problem. Be sure to check your answer.

1. One turkey weighs 16.04 pounds. A second turkey weighs 18.7 pounds. How much more does the heavier turkey weigh?

2. Kayla mixed 1.419 quarts of cranberry juice and 3.785 quarts of apple juice. How many quarts of cranberry-apple punch did she make?

3. Malcolm's turkey should be roasted for 4.5 hours. It has been in the oven 1.7 hours. How much longer must it roast?

4. Melia peeled 4.8 pounds of potatoes. Tara peeled 2.64 pounds. How many pounds of potatoes did they peel together?

5. Drew had 1.67 pounds of carrots. After trimming them, he had 1.5 pounds left. How much did he trim off?

6. A bag of sugar weighed 4.97 pounds. Then Sarah used 0.675 pound to make a pumpkin pie. How much sugar was left in the bag?

7. The Sanchezs' turkey weighed 18.4 pounds. After dinner, only 4.79 pounds of bones were left. How much meat had there been?

8. Pedro poured 0.75 quart of milk into the soup. Later, he added 0.46 quart more milk. How much milk did he put in the soup in all?

Fireworks Family

by Michael Pape

1   Did you ever wonder who makes the fireworks you watch at a baseball game or a July 4th celebration? Fireworks are made all over the world. In many places, they are made by the members of a family, all working together.

2   One American fireworks family is from Bellport, New York. The Grucci family has been making fireworks for more than 140 years. With a lot of hard work and cooperation, uncles, parents, children, and grandchildren create colorful light shows in the sky. The Gruccis make the fireworks for the New York Mets' baseball games. They are also famous for their special effects and the noisy finales of their shows.

3   Like other fireworks families, the Gruccis spend many weeks and months getting ready for a big show. Hundreds and hundreds of fireworks have to be made by hand. Rockets, whistlers, comets, "spider-webs," and flower shapes are just a few of the different kinds of fireworks. The Gruccis like to make fireworks that give a "big bang." One of their biggest was a ball-bomb 24 inches wide. It cost $1,000.00! When it exploded in the sky, the lights spread over a 2,000-foot area.

4   The Gruccis have to plan what kind of show to put on. First, they need to know where the show is to be. Does the show have a special theme? How much money can the customer spend? A special show may need as much as a year to plan well.

5   Packing the fireworks is a very important part of the job of putting on a fireworks show. Because it will be at night, the Gruccis must do their jobs in darkness. Thus, each box of fireworks must have its name marked very clearly. The boxes must all be in order, so the workers don't get mixed up in the dark. The fireworks have to be carefully loaded onto big trucks.

6   During the busy season of July 4th, a big show might take dozens of truckloads of fireworks. On the night of the big show, the hard work pays off. Giant "flowers," rockets, and special effects fill the night. At the end of the show, the many explosions of the finale dazzle the crowd. They clap and whistle and cheer. As the people head home in their cars, the Gruccis are still busy. There's a lot to clean up, and they're already thinking about how to make next year's show even better.

1. What is the main idea of this passage?

   A a family fireworks business

   B New York's fireworks shows

   C how to make fireworks

   D family entertainers

2. **Part A**

   Why does it take the Gruccis so long to get ready for a show?

   A They always have to work in the dark.

   B Most of the fireworks are made by hand.

   C There are many kinds of fireworks.

   D The big trucks drive very slowly.

   Part B

   Underline the sentence in the passage that supports the answer in Part A.

3. When the Gruccis plan a show, they first have to know which of the following?

   A what the biggest bomb will be

   B where the show will be held

   C how many trucks they will need

   D how dark it will be

4. **Part A**

   When does the "finale" of the fireworks show come?

   A when the Gruccis set up

   B before the special effects

   C while the Gruccis are packing

   D at the very end

   Part B

   What helps you know the meaning of the word "finale" in Part A?

   _____

Rachel Carson

1   All things in nature have an effect on one another. Water, air, soil, plants, and animals depend on each other. So when humans damage one part of nature, other parts are often damaged, too. Sometimes there is even damage to humans themselves.

2   Rachel Carson understood these relationships in nature. In her books, she tried to make others understand. She mostly wrote about the sea. But she was also concerned about the land. Her writings have made a valuable contribution to protecting the environment.

3   In the 1950s, farmers in the United States used a spray called DDT on their crops to kill harmful insects. DDT was successful in destroying harmful pests, but it also hurt good insects. The insects carried the DDT in their bodies. When birds ate the insects, they became sick. They laid eggs with very thin and fragile shells. The eggs broke before the baby birds could hatch.

4   In 1962, Rachel Carson wrote the book *Silent Spring.* She explained how DDT and other insect sprays were damaging the environment. She clearly described how the balance of nature was being affected. Other scientists began to learn more about these sprays. And by 1972, the US no longer allowed DDT to be used.

5. What is the author's main purpose for writing this passage?

   A to entertain readers with a story about Rachel Carson and birds

   B to inform people about Rachel Carson's work

   C to debate whether DDT should be used today

   D to persuade people to learn more about Rachel Carson

6. Which sentence from the passage expresses an opinion?

   A "When birds ate the insects, they became sick."

   B "She mostly wrote about the sea."

   C "Her writings have made a valuable contribution to protecting the environment."

   D "Other scientists began to learn more about these sprays."

7. According to the passage, what is *Silent Spring* about?

   A the seasons of the year

   B insect sounds

   C Rachel Carson's life

   D damage to the environment

8. What were two harmful effects of spraying crops with DDT?

   _____

   _____

Mr. Nobody

I know a funny little man,
As quiet as a mouse,
Who does the mischief that is done
In everybody's house!
5 There's no one ever sees his face,
And yet we all agree
That every plate we break was cracked
By Mr. Nobody.

'Tis he who always tears our books
10 Who leaves the door ajar,
He pulls the buttons from our shirts,
And scatters pins afar,
That squeaking door will always squeak
For, pity, don't you see,
15 We leave the oiling to be done
By Mr. Nobody.

The fingermarks on the door
By none of us are made;
We never leave the blinds unclosed,
20 To let the curtains fade.
The ink we never spill, the boots
That lying round you see
Are not our boots; they all belong
To Mr. Nobody.

9. **Part A**

What type of figurative language does the author use in lines 1 and 2?

A metaphor

B alliteration

C simile

D hyperbole

Part B

Underline an example of onomatopoeia in the poem.

10. Why did the author probably write this poem?

    A to encourage people to use a cleaning service

    B to urge people to treat guests with respect

    C to explain why some people believe in ghosts

    D to teach a lesson about personal responsibility

11. What is the tone of this poem?

    A serious

    B humorous

    C sad

    D angry

12. What is the main idea of the poem?

_____

_____

A Friendly Competition

1 Danny and Matt were the best of friends. Usually, it seemed as though nothing would ever come between them. They never fought, and they spent all their free time together. One day, though, something happened that caused quite a conflict between Danny and Matt—they both announced that they wanted to run for student council president.

2 "Danny!" Matt said. "You should not run for president. I would make a much better president."

3 Danny shook his head. "Why? I think I would be a better president!"

4 "Well, we will just see who wins!" Matt said angrily. He set to work making posters. He tried to think of catchy slogans and cool pictures to put on them. He had to think of a way to set himself apart from Danny. They were very similar. Both boys were well-liked by their peers, and both boys were very active on the school basketball team. Matt had to think of a way to make himself stand out. He knew his posters would do the trick, if only he could think of the right things to say on them!

5 While Matt was working on his posters, Danny was busy making buttons. He did not think that posters were the way to go. Instead, he wanted people to wear buttons that said "Vote for Danny!" on them. The buttons were round and white with bright, bold red letters. "These will definitely help me win!" Danny thought.

6 The next day, both boys showed up with the things they had made. Danny's "Vote for Danny" buttons were very popular. Half of the class were wearing them by lunchtime. But the other half of the class were rooting for Matt, whose posters had a lot of bright colors and catchy phrases. While Danny thought simple was best, Matt thought that the only way to win was by impressing everyone with fancy, eye-catching designs.

7 When Danny got home from school that day, he sat down and began to think. He wondered if his buttons were going to be enough. He felt as though he needed something more. He could not do posters, since Matt had already done them. So what could he do that was different?

8 Matt was asking himself the same question at the same time. He was very scared that Danny's buttons were going to outshine his posters. "What am I going to do?" he asked himself. "What am I going to do to make sure I win?"

9 The next day, Matt and Danny arrived at school to find that they had had the same idea: they had both made T-shirts for their campaigns! Matt's said "Vote for Matt!" and Danny's said "Vote for Danny!" The boys tried to be angry with each other at first. "You stole my idea!" Matt yelled.

10 "No! You stole mine!" Danny replied. But, finally, the boys had to laugh. They were too close to allow student council to get in the way. They decided that it did not matter which of them won. They would be happy either way.

11 When the day of the election arrived, the boys wished each other luck. The teacher stepped to the front of the classroom: "Our new student council president will be—" she said. There was a pause. "We have a tie. Danny and Matt! They will share the president's responsibilities."

12 The boys cheered. Neither of them had imagined that they would both win! It did not matter that one of them had used buttons and the other had used posters, and it did not matter that they had had the same idea about T-shirts. Everything had worked out for the best.

13. What caused the conflict between the two boys?

_____

_____

14. One thing that is different between the two boys is that Matt _____.

  A plays basketball

  B runs for president

  C makes buttons

  D makes posters

15. From whose point of view is the story told?

  A Matt's

  B Danny's

  C the teacher's

  D a narrator's

16. Which boy put more into the campaign? Explain.

_____

_____

_____

_____

Writing Midpoint Review

Read the writing prompt below.
Then plan, write, and proofread your answer.
Plan what you are going to write in the space below.
Then write your final answer on another piece of paper.

Suppose your school board is thinking about adding an extra hour to each school day so students can learn more. Do you think this is a good idea? Write a letter to the members of your school board. Be sure to include details and to write it in a way that will convince readers to agree with your opinion.

Math Midpoint Review

1. The call number on a library book is seven hundred forty and eight-hundredths.

   Write this number with numerals.

   _____

2. What number is a factor of 20? Select all that apply.

   A 3

   B 4

   C 5

   D 8

   E 10

   F 30

   G 40

3. Look at the number below.

   1,767,403

   What is the place value of the 6 in this number?

   _____

   How much greater is the 7 farthest to the left than the 7 farthest to the right?

   _____

4. Beth is food shopping. The items in her cart and the costs of each are listed below.

- 1 gallon of milk: $3.59 a gallon
- 1 package of cheese: $2.15 a package
- 2 boxes of cereal: $3.69 a box
- 1 package of meat: $7.49 a package

What is the total amount that Beth will spend on this food?

$ _____

Beth plans to pay for these items with $25.00. How much change should Beth receive?

$ _____

5. Mrs. Stein made 372 cookies to put in gift boxes. She will put 20 cookies in each box.

How many cookies will be left over?

A 2

B 8

C 12

D 18

6. A woodworker makes 238 wooden bowls a month.

At this rate, how many bowls will he make in 12 months?

A 2,746

B 2,756

C 2,846

D 2,856

7. Nick walked 1.525 kilometers from his house to the library. Then he walked 2.36 kilometers from the library to his friend Andy's house. Finally, he walked 2.658 kilometers from Andy's house back to his own home.

   How far did Nick walk in all?

   _____ kilometers

8. Mayuko has oatmeal for breakfast once every 4 days. She has pizza for lunch once every 5 days, and she has ham for dinner once every 8 days.

   How often does Mayuko have oatmeal, pizza, and ham on the same day?

   A   once every 20 days

   B   once every 40 days

   C   once every 80 days

   D   once every 160 days

9. Which list shows all the prime numbers between 20 and 40?

   A   23, 29, 31, 37

   B   23, 27, 29, 31, 37

   C   21, 23, 29, 31, 37, 39

   D   21, 23, 27, 29, 31, 37, 39

10. Which of the following is true? Select all that apply.

   A $3.76 > 3.67$

   B $2.59 < 2.510$

   C $7.008 < 7.08$

   D $4.416 > 4.423$

   E $5.834 < 5.743$

   F $1.385 > 1.375$

11. Tyrell had $73.52. He then spent $42.73 on a pair of shoes.

    Which is the best estimate of the amount of money Tyrell had left?

    A $20

    B $30

    C $40

    D $50

12. Find the product.

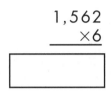

13. The numbers of people at five hockey games are shown below.

HOCKEY GAME ATTENDANCE

Game	Number of People
1	8,954
2	8,477
3	9,658
4	7,912
5	8,743

Of these games, write the games with the three greatest numbers of people in order from least to greatest.

_____

The average attendance for this team's games is 8,859. Which games had less than the average attendance?

_____

14. Jade purchased a CD for $14.65, including the tax.

    How much change did she get from a twenty-dollar bill?

    A $5.35

    B $5.45

    C $6.35

    D $6.45

15. A truck carried a load of TV sets that weighed a total of 6,496 pounds. Each TV set weighed 28 pounds.

    How many TV sets was the truck carrying?

    A   232

    B   267

    C   308

    D   332

16. The lengths of some cross-country ski trails are shown in the table below.

SKI TRAIL LENGTHS

Trail	Length (in miles)
Peak	3.65
Valley	3.092
Lake	4.275
Moon	3.25
Sunset	4.355

Which of the following statements is true? Select all that apply.

    A   Valley is the longest trail.

    B   Peak is longer than Moon.

    C   Lake is the shortest trail.

    D   Sunset is longer than Lake.

    E   Moon and Peak are the same length.

    F   Peak is longer than Valley.

17. Lisa is going to display 72 arrowheads in a museum display. She will put them in equal rows.

How many arrowheads could be in each row? Select all that apply.

    A 24

    B 16

    C 14

    D 12

    E 9

    F 7

18. Find the quotient.

$$24 \overline{)6{,}495}$$ R

SENTENCE FRAGMENTS

A **sentence** tells a complete thought. It has a subject and a predicate.

Cross out each group of words below that is not a sentence.
Put the correct punctuation mark at the end of each sentence.

1. Is in northern China

2. The wall runs from west to east

3. Built to keep China safe from attack

4. Emperor to join walls already standing into one wall

5. Parts of wall built at different times

6. Took 1,000 years to build wall we see today

7. Some areas are only 2 feet tall

8. The most visited part of the wall is 6 feet tall

9. Stretches more than 4,500 miles

10. It runs through mountains, deserts, and grassland

11. Looks like a snake

12. The Great Wall of China is so long it can be seen from space

13. Watchtowers were built into the wall

14. Some of the wall is crumbling today

15. The wall is built of bricks and mortar

MULTIPLYING AND DIVIDING DECIMALS BY TENS

To multiply a decimal by—

    10, move the decimal point **one** place to the right. $10 \times 2.35 = 23.5$

    100, move the decimal point **two** places to the right. $100 \times 2.35 = 235.0$

    1,000, move the decimal point **three** places to the right. $1,000 \times 2.35 = 2,350.0$

Write zeros in the product if you need them to place the decimal point.

Multiply.

1. $10 \times 6.32 = $ _____

2. $0.875 \times 10 = $ _____

3. $100 \times 7.47 = $ _____

4. $0.036 \times 1,000 = $ _____

5. $5.03 \times 10 = $ _____

6. $1,000 \times 6.988 = $ _____

7. $100 \times 0.549 = $ _____

8. $10 \times 0.031 = $ _____

9. $1.904 \times 100 = $ _____

10. $9.7 \times 1,000 = $ _____

11. $200.86 \times 10 = $ _____

12. $357.992 \times 100 = $ _____

To divide a decimal by—

    10, move the decimal point **one** place to the left. $2.35 \div 10 = 0.235$

    100, move the decimal point **two** places to the left. $2.35 \div 100 = 0.0235$

    1,000, move the decimal point **three** places to the left. $2.35 \div 1,000 = 0.00235$

Write zeros in the product if you need them to place the decimal point.

Divide.

13. $6.58 \div 10 = $ _____

14. $27.84 \div 100 = $ _____

15. $7,925.1 \div 1,000 = $ _____

16. $0.415 \div 10 = $ _____

17. $371.57 \div 100 = $ _____

18. $28.9 \div 1,000 = $ _____

19. $529.6 \div 10 = $ _____

20. $8.324 \div 100 = $ _____

21. $153.225 \div 1,000 = $ _____

22. $90.525 \div 10 = $ _____

23. $4.6 \div 100 = $ _____

24. $1.78 \div 1,000 = $ _____

RUN-ON SENTENCES

Divide each group of words into two sentences. Circle each small letter that should be a capital letter. Put the correct punctuation mark at the end of each sentence.

1. pandas like to eat bamboo it grows in warm areas

2. four quarts equal one gallon what equals a pint

3. watch out there is paint on the floor

4. our team is up to bat what is the score

5. do you play a musical instrument i have always wanted to play the piano

6. i forgot to have you sign the form where did i put it

7. can you read that sign from here what does it say

8. the bald eagle flies fast it is a symbol of strength

9. jenn chose the paint herself the room looks very different

10. the captain spoke to his troops he ordered them to capture the fort

11. what a colorful sunset there's no place like the West

12. this looks like a good spot for fishing let's anchor here

13. would you like some peas may i have the chicken

14. we went to the concert the singer was very good

15. how much do the sodas cost i would like two

MULTIPLICATION WITH DECIMALS

When you multiply decimals, the product should have the same number of decimal places as the total number of decimal places in both factors.
Multiply.

1. 4.3
    ×7

2. 8.1
    ×5

3. 25.8
    ×3

4. 1.2
    ×44

5. 71.4
    ×26

6. 5.63
    ×4

7. 2.42
    ×9

8. 19.08
    ×5

9. 3.87
    ×13

10. 28.11
     ×45

11. 76
     ×0.3

12. 25
     ×0.7

13. 59
     ×8.2

14. 32
     ×0.19

15. 94
     ×0.25

16. 2.6
     ×0.4

17. 4.8
     ×0.6

18. 7.1
     ×0.2

19. 5.3
     ×1.6

20. 13.9
     ×6.8

Find the answer to each word problem.

21. A sheet of paper is 8.5 inches wide. If 5 sheets are taped together side to side, how wide will the combined sheets be?

22. A large muffin weighs 6.3 ounces. If Charlie eats 1.5 muffins, how many ounces does he eat?

AVOIDING DOUBLE NEGATIVES

Use only one negative word in a sentence. Negative words are words that mean <u>no</u> or <u>not</u>, including contractions made with <u>not</u>.

I can <u>never</u> find any clean clothes.
or

I <u>can't</u> ever find any clean clothes.
not

I <u>can't</u> <u>never</u> find <u>no</u> clean clothes.

Underline the negative words in each sentence. Then rewrite each sentence, using only one negative word.

1. My mom says I shouldn't never leave my clothes on the floor.

   _____

2. She can't find no place to walk in my room.

   _____

3. Nobody can't come into my room until I clean it.

   _____

4. I needed clean socks, but I couldn't find none.

   _____

5. Soon, I won't have nothing clean to wear.

   _____

6. I don't have nowhere to put things in my closet.

   _____

7. After I'm finished cleaning, you won't find a cleaner room nowhere.

   _____

DIVISION WITH DECIMALS

Dividing decimals is like dividing whole numbers. When a decimal is divided by a whole number, the decimal point is placed in the quotient directly above its original position.

Place the decimal point correctly in each quotient.

1. $8\overline{)68.8}$ 8 6

2. $33\overline{)303.6}$ 9 2

3. $21\overline{)15.96}$ 0 76

4. $5\overline{)0.145}$ 0 029

Divide. Remember to place zeros in the quotient where necessary.

5. $4\overline{)3.84}$

6. $9\overline{)15.3}$

7. $3\overline{)0.168}$

8. $8\overline{)0.072}$

9. $26\overline{)33.8}$

10. $15\overline{)0.525}$

11. $78\overline{)2.262}$

12. $92\overline{)7.36}$

13. Ms. Atkinson sold 13.25 acres of land. If it was divided into 5 equal-sized parts, how big was each part?

14. A bag of candy weighs 2.88 pounds. If it holds 32 pieces of the same size, how much does each piece weigh?

15. In 7 days, a total of 5.95 inches of rain fell. What was the average amount of rain that fell per day?

SHORT FORMS

The first true airplane flight was made on _____ 17, 1903.
(December)

It was made by _____ Orville Wright at Kitty Hawk,
(Mister)

_____. The plane _____ go very far. It only flew
(North Carolina)   (did not)

120 _____.
(feet)

Planes _____ really important until World War I. By the
(were not)

1920s, _____ become much more familiar. And in 1927,
(they had)

Charles _____ Lindbergh became a national hero by
(Augustus)

flying from New York to Paris without stopping. The trip was

3,600 _____ long. When Lindbergh returned to the
(miles)

_____, _____ Calvin Coolidge gave him
(United States)   (President)

a medal.

In 1932, another pilot became famous. Her friends called her

_____. She flew alone across the Atlantic Ocean in
(Amelia Earhart)

15 _____ and 18 _____.
(hours)   (minutes)

EQUIVALENT FRACTIONS

Write equivalent fractions.

1.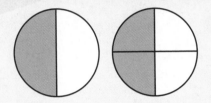

$$\frac{1}{2} = \frac{1 \times 2}{2 \times 2} = \frac{}{4}$$

2.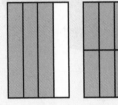

$$\frac{3}{4} = \frac{3 \times}{4 \times} = \frac{}{8}$$

3.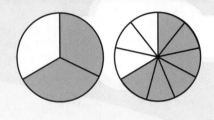

$$\frac{2}{3} = \frac{2 \times}{3 \times} = \frac{}{9}$$

4. $\frac{1}{2} = \frac{1 \times 4}{2 \times 4} = \frac{}{8}$

5. $\frac{2}{5} = \frac{2 \times}{5 \times 2} = \frac{}{10}$

6. $\frac{5}{7} = \frac{5 \times}{7 \times} = \frac{}{21}$

7. $\frac{3}{4} = \frac{}{12}$

8. $\frac{2}{9} = \frac{}{18}$

9. $\frac{4}{5} = \frac{}{15}$

10. $\frac{1}{2} = \frac{}{14}$

11. $\frac{5}{6} = \frac{}{24}$

12. $\frac{2}{3} = \frac{}{12}$

13. $\frac{3}{4} = \frac{}{16}$

14. $\frac{1}{2} = \frac{}{10}$

15. $\frac{3}{8} = \frac{}{24}$

16. $\frac{4}{5} = \frac{}{20}$

Write equivalent fractions with the same denominators for each pair of fractions below.

17. $\frac{1}{2} = \frac{}{6}$

$\frac{1}{3} = \frac{}{6}$

18. $\frac{3}{5} = \frac{}{10}$

$\frac{1}{2} = \frac{}{\text{—}}$

19. $\frac{2}{3} = \frac{}{12}$

$\frac{3}{4} = \frac{}{\text{—}}$

20. $\frac{3}{5} = \frac{}{15}$

$\frac{1}{3} = \frac{}{\text{—}}$

21. $\frac{5}{6} = \frac{}{18}$

$\frac{7}{9} = \frac{}{\text{—}}$

Complete each problem with an equivalent fraction.

22. Stella watered $\frac{1}{3}$ of the plants. She watered $\frac{}{36}$ of them.

23. Hitoshi sold $\frac{5}{8}$ of the trees on sale at the nursery. He sold $\frac{}{24}$ of the trees.

COMPREHENSION: LITERARY ELEMENTS

Read the passage. Then answer the questions.

Grounded

by Simon Rogers

1 It's a beautiful day, and I'm stuck inside. Why? Well, it's all because of last weekend.

2 My friends and I decided to play baseball. Six of us got together and walked to the park down the street. We were going to use the baseball diamond there. Unfortunately, when we got there, there were already a bunch of kids playing. We didn't know any of them, so we decided to play somewhere else.

3 "Where else is there to play?" my friends asked. We couldn't think of a baseball diamond that was close enough to walk to.

4 "Wait a minute," my friend Jackie said to me. "Don't you have a pretty big backyard? Can't we play there?"

5 I stuttered and tried to think of an excuse. My parents always told me never to play baseball in the backyard because they were worried I'd break one of our windows—or worse, one of the neighbors' windows. But I was too embarrassed to tell my friends that my parents wouldn't let me. And, since my parents were visiting family that afternoon, I decided to let my friends come over. "Okay," I said. "We have to be careful, though. My yard isn't exactly huge, and I wouldn't want to break a window."

6 With that, we walked to my house. We got ready to play our three-on-three game. "All right," I said. "The bush here will be home plate, that tree will be first base, and we'll use rocks for second and third base. Remember, everyone. Please be careful!"

7 "We will!" my friends shouted at me. "Come on—let's play!" I took a deep breath. I looked around my backyard, and I looked at all the windows on my house. I hoped everything would be okay.

8 We played for about half an hour, and everything seemed to be going well. No balls had even gone near the house. Finally, it was my turn at bat. My friend Brian was pitching. He's a really good baseball player, so I never expected to hit the ball when he was pitching. Sure enough, his first pitch flew right past me. Strike one. The next one sailed past me, too. Strike two. But the next pitch was not as fast, and when I swung the bat with all my might, I made contact.

9 "Yes!" I cried. And then I heard the terrible sound: glass shattering. "Oh, no!" I yelled. "Tell me it's not what I think it is." But it was. My friends and I looked at my kitchen window, which now was in pieces. My parents would surely know how the hole got there, and if they didn't, the neighbors would surely tell them we were playing baseball.

10 "Okay guys," I said. I tried to be cool. "Game over. I have to clean up the glass and call my parents."

11 "Sorry," my friends muttered as they left. I ran inside. There was a shattered window, glass all over the kitchen floor, and my parents were going to be home any minute. I used a broom to clean up the glass as quickly as I could, but I could not hide the window. When my parents got home, I told them what had happened. I explained that I had felt pressure to let my friends play in our backyard, even though I had been told not to.

12 "Well," my dad said, "I'm sorry you felt that pressure. You still broke rules, though, and that is not okay." I got grounded for a month. So, here I am, sitting inside on a beautiful spring day. Next time, I'll follow the rules. Looks as though it's time to find a new baseball field.

1. What does paragraph 1 of the story mainly introduce?

   A theme   C flashback

   B setting   D characters

2. What is the point of view of the story?

   A first person

   B third-person limited

   C third-person objective

   D third-person omniscient

3. With which paragraph does the flashback in the story end?

   A paragraph 1

   B paragraph 4

   C paragraph 8

   D paragraph 12

4. **Part A**

   Which word best describes the main character's dad as presented in the story?

   A cruel   C giving

   B fair   D awkward

   Part B

   Which line or lines from the story best supports your answer to Part A?

   A "I stuttered and tried to think of an excuse."

   B "'I'm sorry you felt that pressure. You still broke rules, though, and that is not okay.'"

   C "When my parents got home, I told them what had happened."

   D "But I was too embarrassed to tell my friends that my parents wouldn't let me."

5. Answer the following question on a separate piece of paper.

   How does the setting of the story contribute to the conflict of the story? Explain.

SIMPLIFYING FRACTIONS

Write an equivalent fraction in lower terms.

1. $\dfrac{16}{28} = \dfrac{16 \div 2}{28 \div 2} = \dfrac{}{14}$

2. $\dfrac{8}{12} = \dfrac{8 \div}{12 \div} = \dfrac{}{6}$

3. $\dfrac{6}{18} = \dfrac{6 \div}{18 \div} = \dfrac{}{6}$

4. $\dfrac{18}{24} = \dfrac{}{8}$

5. $\dfrac{16}{20} = \dfrac{}{10}$

6. $\dfrac{24}{36} = \dfrac{}{9}$

7. $\dfrac{32}{48} = \dfrac{}{12}$

8. $\dfrac{42}{56} = \dfrac{}{8}$

Write an equivalent fraction in lowest terms.

9. $\dfrac{8}{12} = \dfrac{8 \div}{12 \div} = \dfrac{}{3}$

10. $\dfrac{6}{24} = \dfrac{6 \div}{24 \div} = \dfrac{}{4}$

11. $\dfrac{12}{20} = \dfrac{12 \div}{20 \div} = \dfrac{}{5}$

12. $\dfrac{6}{12} = \dfrac{}{2}$

13. $\dfrac{3}{24} = \dfrac{}{8}$

14. $\dfrac{12}{15} = \dfrac{}{5}$

15. $\dfrac{9}{12} = \dfrac{}{4}$

16. $\dfrac{6}{36} = \dfrac{}{6}$

17. $\dfrac{12}{16} = -$

18. $\dfrac{5}{10} = -$

19. $\dfrac{20}{30} = -$

20. $\dfrac{10}{25} = -$

21. $\dfrac{16}{48} = -$

22. $\dfrac{16}{24} = -$

23. $\dfrac{21}{28} = -$

24. $\dfrac{24}{40} = -$

25. $\dfrac{20}{32} = -$

26. $\dfrac{36}{42} = -$

Complete each problem with an equivalent fraction in lowest terms.

27. On Karina's map, $\dfrac{10}{16}$ inch represents one mile. In other words, — inch equals one mile.

28. Andre lives $\dfrac{8}{10}$ mile from his best friend, Elijah. Elijah lives — mile away.

FRACTIONS AND DECIMALS

You can show fractions as decimals and some decimals as fractions.
Write an equivalent fraction with a denominator of 100. Add the decimal point.

$$\frac{12}{25} = \frac{48}{100} = 0.48 \qquad\qquad \frac{2}{5} = \frac{40}{100} = 0.4$$

Write the decimal as a fraction with a denominator of 100. Simplify, if possible.

Write the correct fraction and decimal for each figure or set below.

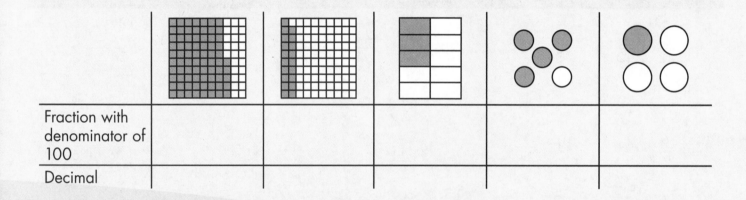

Fraction with denominator of 100					
Decimal					

Write each decimal as a fraction in lowest terms.

1. 0.64 =

2. 0.9 =

3. 0.42 =

4. 0.38 =

5. 0.06 =

6. 0.26 =

7. 0.2 =

8. 0.55 =

9. 0.18 =

Write each fraction as an equivalent fraction with a denominator of 100 and as a decimal.

10. $\frac{3}{4}$ =

11. $\frac{4}{10}$ =

12. $\frac{1}{2}$ =

13. $\frac{5}{20}$ =

14. $\frac{7}{10}$ =

15. $\frac{3}{5}$ =

16. $\frac{14}{20}$ =

17. $\frac{4}{5}$ =

18. $\frac{6}{25}$ =

CONTRACTIONS

A **contraction** is two words written together with one or more letters left out. An apostrophe takes the place of the missing letters.

were not ⟶ weren't   I would ⟶ I'd

Write a contraction for the words in parentheses to complete each sentence.

1. My brother _____ playing in the game. But I _____ know why.
   (is not)   (do not)

2. The doctor _____ know what is wrong with my ankle yet. He _____
   (does not)   (will not)
   know until we get an x-ray.

3. _____ you going to the library with me? _____ be leaving soon.
   (Are not)   (I will)

4. Karen _____ ready. She _____ find her mittens and hat.
   (was not)   (could not)

5. _____ let the cats out. _____ run away.
   (Do not)   (They will)

6. The campers _____ gone to bed yet. _____ been listening to
   (have not)   (They have)
   scary stories.

7. _____ Asad call? _____ supposed to tell us where to meet him.
   (Did not)   (He is)

8. Why _____ you resting? _____ not doing what the doctor said.
   (are not)   (You are)

9. I _____ say who will win the contest. _____ too soon to tell.
   (can not)   (It is)

10. _____ going to the shore next week. _____ really looking forward to it.
    (We are)   (I am)

ADDING AND SUBTRACTING UNLIKE FRACTIONS

1. $\dfrac{1}{8} + \dfrac{1}{4} =$

$\dfrac{1}{8} + \dfrac{1 \times \boxed{}}{4 \times \boxed{}} =$

$\dfrac{1}{8} + \dfrac{}{8} = \dfrac{}{8}$

2. $\dfrac{1}{2} - \dfrac{3}{8} =$

$\dfrac{1 \times \boxed{}}{2 \times \boxed{}} - \dfrac{3}{8} =$

$\dfrac{}{8} - \dfrac{3}{8} = \dfrac{}{8}$

3. $\dfrac{2}{3} + \dfrac{1}{9} =$

$\dfrac{2 \times \boxed{}}{3 \times \boxed{}} + \dfrac{1}{9} =$

$\dfrac{}{9} + \dfrac{}{9} = \dfrac{}{9}$

4. $\dfrac{1}{12} + \dfrac{5}{6} =$

5. $\dfrac{1}{2} + \dfrac{1}{8} =$

6. $\dfrac{1}{4} + \dfrac{1}{12} =$

7. $\dfrac{3}{8} - \dfrac{1}{4} =$

8. $\dfrac{1}{3} - \dfrac{2}{9} =$

9. $\dfrac{14}{15} - \dfrac{2}{3} =$

10. $\begin{aligned} \dfrac{4}{15} &= \\ + \dfrac{2}{5} &= \\ \hline \end{aligned}$

11. $\begin{aligned} \dfrac{3}{4} \\ - \dfrac{1}{2} \\ \hline \end{aligned}$

12. $\begin{aligned} \dfrac{5}{9} \\ - \dfrac{1}{3} \\ \hline \end{aligned}$

13. $\begin{aligned} \dfrac{7}{10} \\ - \dfrac{1}{2} \\ \hline \end{aligned}$

14. $\begin{aligned} \dfrac{7}{9} \\ + \dfrac{1}{18} \\ \hline \end{aligned}$

15. $\begin{aligned} \dfrac{5}{12} \\ + \dfrac{1}{2} \\ \hline \end{aligned}$

ISN'T AND AREN'T, WASN'T AND WEREN'T

Isn't is the contraction for is not. Use it with a singular subject. Aren't is the contraction for are not. Use it with a plural subject or the pronoun you. Wasn't is the contraction for was not. Use it with a singular subject. Weren't is the contraction for were not. Use it with a plural subject or the pronoun you.

Circle the correct word to complete each sentence.

1. Finding treasure on the beach _____ easy. Coins and jewelry
   isn't   aren't

   _____ lying near the surface. Shovels _____ the best tool to use,
   isn't   aren't   isn't   aren't

   either. But often it _____ possible to use anything else.
                        isn't   aren't

2. It _____ a good idea to get too close to a rhinoceros. But wildlife experts
      isn't   aren't

   _____ giving up on saving these animals. Many Asians and Middle Easterners
   isn't   aren't

   _____ willing to stop buying rhinoceros horns. It _____ hard to see
   wasn't   weren't   wasn't   weren't

   that the animals would have to be protected.

3. The automobile _____ widely used in America until after 1910. Many of the
                   wasn't   weren't

   early manufacturers _____ successful. Assembly lines _____
                       wasn't   weren't   wasn't   weren't

   introduced by Henry Ford until 1913. It _____ long after that that Detroit became
                                           wasn't   weren't

   the automobile capital of the world.

PROBLEM SOLVING: ADDING AND SUBTRACTING UNLIKE FRACTIONS

Find the answer to each word problem. Write each answer in lowest terms.

1. Mrs. Diaz had $\frac{5}{6}$ gallon of paint to start. When she finished, she had $\frac{1}{3}$ gallon. How much paint did she use?

2. A farmer sold $\frac{1}{2}$ of his turkeys at Thanksgiving and $\frac{3}{8}$ of them at Christmas. What part of his turkeys did he sell?

3. John ate $\frac{1}{6}$ of the cake and Mike ate $\frac{1}{12}$ of it. How much of the cake did the two boys eat?

4. Ms. Bahn had $\frac{3}{4}$ of a tank of gas in her car. Then she used $\frac{1}{8}$ of a tank. How much gas did she have left?

5. Mr. Shaw spends $\frac{1}{5}$ of his pay on rent and $\frac{1}{15}$ on food. What part of his pay does he spend on rent and food?

6. Vikram spent $\frac{1}{3}$ hour walking his dog and $\frac{3}{6}$ hour playing fetch. How much more time did he spend playing fetch?

7. A printer holds $\frac{9}{10}$ of a pack of paper. Portia uses $\frac{3}{20}$ of a pack. What part of a pack is left in the printer?

8. Neela spent $\frac{5}{12}$ hour on math homework and $\frac{1}{4}$ hour on science homework. How much time did she spend on both?

HOMOPHONES

Homophones are words that sound the same but are spelled differently and have different meanings.

sail

sale

Circle the word in each list that is a homophone for the underlined word at the top of the list.

1. road
   row
   rode
   rope

2. week
   wood
   well
   weak

3. ate
   arm
   eight
   eye

4. knew
   king
   new
   none

5. hole
   wheel
   hall
   whole

6. pail
   pale
   pool
   pair

7. by
   bike
   buy
   boy

8. flower
   fly
   flame
   flour

Circle the correct homophone to complete each sentence.

9. If you can ⟮write / right⟯ the answer, raise your ⟮write / right⟯ hand.

10. Which ⟮weigh / way⟯ is that elephant going, and how much does it ⟮weigh / way⟯?

11. We can only park ⟮hour / our⟯ car here for an ⟮hour / our⟯.

MIXED NUMBERS AND IMPROPER FRACTIONS

Write mixed numbers and improper fractions for the shaded parts.

1.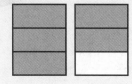

_____

2.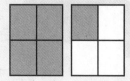

_____

3.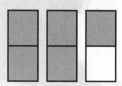

_____

Change each mixed number to an improper fraction.

4. $1\frac{1}{2} = \frac{}{2} + \frac{}{2} = \frac{}{2}$

5. $2\frac{3}{4} = \frac{}{4} + \frac{}{4} = \frac{}{4}$

6. $1\frac{3}{5} =$

7. $2\frac{7}{9} =$

Multiply. Write each mixed number as an improper fraction.

8. $2\frac{1}{3} = \frac{(\quad \times \quad) +}{3} =$

9. $2\frac{1}{2} = \frac{(\quad \times \quad) +}{2} =$

10. $\frac{4}{3} = \frac{}{3} + \frac{}{3} =$

11. $\frac{5}{2} = \frac{}{2} + \frac{}{2} =$

12. $\frac{9}{2} =$

13. $\frac{10}{3} =$

Divide. Write each answer as a mixed number.

14. $\frac{7}{2} = 2\overline{)7}$

15. $\frac{5}{3} =$

16. $\frac{12}{5} =$

Find the answer to each word problem.

17. A camp cook used $3\frac{1}{3}$ boxes of pancake mix at breakfast. What is this number as an improper fraction?

18. Paul practiced his lines for a play for $\frac{7}{4}$ hours. What is this fraction as a mixed number?

HOMOPHONES

Homophones are words that sound the same but are spelled differently and have different meanings.

they're = they are   there = in that place   their = belonging to them

Write they're, there, or their to complete each sentence correctly.

1. The twins are over _____ by the pond.

2. _____ putting on _____ skates.

3. Do you see _____ jackets?

4. _____ thick and warm.

5. The ice looks thin over _____ near the sign.

6. Josh and Joel will watch _____ younger brother.

7. He might fall in if _____ not watching him.

8. Josh is warning his brother not to go _____.

ADDING AND SUBTRACTING MIXED NUMBERS

1. $6\frac{3}{8} =$
$+8\frac{1}{4} =$

2. $1\frac{1}{3}$
$+9\frac{5}{12}$

3. $9\frac{3}{10}$
$+4\frac{1}{2}$

4. $8\frac{11}{12} =$
$-6\frac{1}{4} =$

5. $9\frac{5}{6}$
$-2\frac{1}{2}$

6. 8
$-2\frac{2}{3}$

7. $4\frac{7}{15}$
$+2\frac{4}{5}$

8. $2\frac{2}{3}$
$+7\frac{5}{9}$

9. $2\frac{1}{2}$
$+2\frac{3}{6}$

10. $3\frac{1}{4}$
$-1\frac{1}{3}$

11. $2\frac{7}{15}$
$-1\frac{4}{5}$

12. $5\frac{1}{6}$
$-\ \ \frac{2}{3}$

Find the answer to each word problem. Write your answer in lowest terms.

13. Miguel made 5 gallons of chili for a party. His guests ate $4\frac{3}{16}$ gallons. How much chili was left?

14. The drive from Nicole's house to the airport took $1\frac{5}{6}$ hours. From her arrival to her landing took $5\frac{2}{3}$ hours. How long did the trip take in all?

COMPREHENSION: AUTHOR'S PURPOSE

Read the passage. Then answer the questions.

1   As the teacher told us how much we would be helping our school, all I could think about was that pirate hat I wanted. It was big, black, and had a mean-looking skull and bones on the front. If I sold ten magazine subscriptions, I could win that pirate hat. After school that day, I grabbed my pen, magazine sales catalog, and order form sheet. The first stop was my aunt's house.

2   Aunt Rosa lived just down the block from me. My aunt loved me, and I was sure she would like to help my school. Aunt Rosa let me in, and then she offered me milk and cookies. I wanted to be quick so that I could make more sales. But I could not turn down her homemade cookies. So I sat with Aunt Rosa and told her about school. Then I began telling her about the magazine subscriptions that I wanted to sell her. Aunt Rosa said she wanted to help, but she already had many magazines that she didn't read. She said that she put them in the garbage more than she read them. I looked around, and I saw many craft magazines sitting in a pile. Aunt Rosa had arthritis in her hands. It had gotten so bad that she could barely even cook. I thanked her for the cookies, and I headed on my way.

3   My next stop was Aunt Tina. She lived five blocks away. So I had to ride my bicycle there. My Aunt Tina was my mother's sister, and my Aunt Rosa was my father's sister. So they really didn't even know each other. But, boy, they both made good cookies. My Aunt Tina offered me some cookies and milk, as Aunt Rosa had. I told her about my magazine subscriptions. Aunt Tina said she was interested in craft magazines. I got very excited, for this could be my first sale. I would be only nine more sales away from my pirate hat.

4   Aunt Tina asked how much the crafting magazine was. I told her that one was $19.95. She said that she could not afford that magazine right now. I felt very bad because I knew she was right. Both of her sons were in college, and it was hard for her to pay for their tuition. Just then, I had an idea. Aunt Rosa had all those crafting magazines that she threw away. Aunt Tina could use those magazines.

5   I told my Aunt Tina that I could give her some magazines for free. Aunt Tina was very excited. She loved to make crafts, but she was running out of ideas. So I rode my bike to Aunt Rosa's, and I got the magazines that she wanted to throw away. I rode them over to Aunt Tina's. I showed Aunt Tina the pirate hat that I had hoped to win. Aunt Tina showed me that there was a pattern for just the hat I wanted. I didn't sell any magazines that day, but I got my pirate hat a few weeks later. It was the best pirate hat I had ever seen. It was better than I had dreamed because my Aunt Tina made it all by herself.

1. What is the author's purpose in this selection?

   A   to teach how to make a magazine sale

   B   to describe how to make a pirate hat

   C   to tell an amusing story about a young boy

   D   to inform about different kinds of magazines

2. **Part A**

   Which of these is an opinion expressed in the passage?

   A   "If I sold ten magazine subscriptions, I could win that pirate hat."

   B   "Aunt Rosa lived just down the block from me."

   C   "Aunt Rosa had arthritis in her hands."

   D   "It was the best pirate hat I had ever seen."

   Part B

   Which of these is a fact expressed in the passage?

   A   "It was big, black, and had a mean-looking skull and bones on the front."

   B   "If I sold ten magazine subscriptions, I could win that pirate hat."

   C   "It was better than I had dreamed because my Aunt Tina made it all by herself."

   D   "But, boy, they both made good cookies."

3. What is the author's main purpose in paragraph 1?

   A   to describe the magazine subscriptions in detail

   B   to explain who the narrator's aunts were

   C   to describe the narrator's excitement over winning a pirate hat

   D   to persuade readers that everyone should sell magazines

4. Who is the intended audience of this passage?

   A   general readers

   B   people who enjoy doing crafts

   C   schools that are planning fundraisers

   D   students who are selling magazine subscriptions

5. Answer the following question on a separate piece of paper.

   What is the tone of this selection? How does the tone help you understand the author's purpose?

PROBLEM SOLVING: ADDING AND SUBTRACTING MIXED NUMBERS

Find the answer to each word problem. Write your answer in lowest terms.

1. A puppy weighs $10\frac{1}{4}$ pounds. It weighed $7\frac{1}{2}$ pounds last week. How much weight has it gained?

2. It rained $6\frac{1}{2}$ inches in May and $5\frac{5}{6}$ inches in June. How much did it rain altogether in these two months?

3. Mrs. Webster bought 12 yards of rope. She used only $9\frac{1}{6}$ yards. How much rope did she have left over?

4. Cal ran the first race in $11\frac{1}{5}$ seconds and the next race in $12\frac{1}{10}$ seconds. How long did he run in both races?

5. Vijay worked for $3\frac{1}{4}$ hours. Sita worked for $2\frac{5}{12}$ hours. How much longer did Vijay work than Sita?

6. Yonit sang one song that was $3\frac{1}{2}$ minutes long. Her second song was $2\frac{2}{3}$ minutes long. How long did Yonit sing in all?

7. An aquarium held 10 gallons of water. It sprang a leak. Only $4\frac{3}{8}$ gallons of water remained. How much water leaked out?

8. Toby used $1\frac{1}{4}$ yards of black cloth and $1\frac{5}{6}$ yards of green cloth for a costume. How much fabric did he use in all?

ADDING AND SUBTRACTING FRACTIONS AND MIXED NUMBERS

Add or subtract. Write each answer in lowest terms.

1. $\frac{1}{4}$
$+\frac{3}{7}$

2. $5\frac{1}{3}$
$-2\frac{2}{3}$

3. $4\frac{3}{8}$
$+2\frac{3}{8}$

4. $\frac{17}{24}$
$+\frac{1}{6}$

5. $2\frac{1}{12}$
$-\frac{5}{6}$

6. $\frac{5}{16}$
$+\frac{7}{16}$

7. $6\frac{1}{3}$
$+1\frac{4}{15}$

8. $3\frac{1}{6}$
$-2\frac{5}{8}$

9. $\frac{13}{18}$
$-\frac{2}{9}$

10. $\frac{3}{4}$
$+\frac{3}{8}$

11. $3\frac{7}{20}$
$-\frac{1}{4}$

12. $\frac{2}{3}$
$-\frac{1}{2}$

13. $2\frac{1}{6}$
$-1\frac{5}{9}$

14. $1\frac{7}{24}$
$+2\frac{14}{24}$

15. $4\frac{2}{5}$
$-1\frac{1}{2}$

16. $4\frac{3}{4}$
$+3\frac{3}{5}$

17. Daria fed her dog $\frac{3}{4}$ pound of canned food and $1\frac{1}{3}$ pounds of dry food today. How much food was that in all?

18. Boris opened a 50-pound bag of puppy food. The puppies ate $10\frac{1}{5}$ pounds of it in two days. How much food was left in the bag?

PREFIXES

Each of these **prefixes** means "not": <u>in</u>-, <u>non</u>-, <u>dis</u>-, and <u>un</u>-. The spelling of <u>in</u>- is changed to <u>im</u>- before words that begin with <u>m</u>, <u>b</u>, or <u>p</u>.
The prefixes <u>un</u>- and <u>dis</u>- can also mean "the opposite of" the word to which they are added.

Complete each sentence below by adding one of the above prefixes to each incomplete word.

1. There are very few vegetables that Connie _____ likes.

2. Miguel sent me a message written in _____ visible ink.

3. The old coin was _____ like any other I'd ever seen.

4. The campers could not drink the water because it was _____ pure.

5. I was amazed when the magician made the elephant _____ appear.

6. We arrived at the meeting late because we took an _____ direct route.

7. Aunt Martha paid us an _____ expected visit yesterday.

8. Lan became _____ patient when her car would not start.

9. If you _____ agree with the new rule, tell me your reasons.

10. The train traveled _____ stop from Washington, DC, to New York City.

11. It is _____ polite to eat food with a knife.

12. Gerry had only one _____ correct answer on his test.

13. Pioneers are thrilled with thoughts of the _____ known.

14. I like the taste of _____ fat milk.

15. To me, believing in ghosts is _____ sense.

16. The _____ complete game will be finished next week.

17. How can I _____ lock the door if I've lost the key?

18. Kevin was _____ pleased with his science grade.

MULTIPLICATION AND FRACTIONS

1. $\frac{1}{2} \times 8 =$

2. $9 \times \frac{1}{3} =$

3. $\frac{1}{4} \times 20 =$

4. $9 \times \frac{2}{3} =$

5. $\frac{1}{8} \times 16 =$

6. $12 \times \frac{5}{6} =$

7. $\frac{3}{8} \times 16 =$

8. $36 \times \frac{2}{9} =$

9. $\frac{1}{5} \times 15 =$

10. $\frac{3}{8} \times \frac{2}{3} =$

11. $\frac{3}{4} \times \frac{3}{4} =$

12. $\frac{7}{8} \times \frac{1}{4} =$

13. $\frac{1}{8} \times \frac{4}{5} =$

14. $\frac{1}{3} \times \frac{1}{9} =$

15. $\frac{6}{7} \times \frac{2}{3} =$

16. $\frac{3}{4} \times \frac{5}{6} =$

17. $\frac{5}{8} \times \frac{2}{5} =$

18. $\frac{1}{3} \times \frac{3}{4} =$

Solve.

19. Zareh had 4 gallons of paint. She used $\frac{1}{2}$ of that amount to paint a room. How many gallons did she use?

20. Gavin had $\frac{5}{6}$ quart of brush cleaner. He used $\frac{2}{3}$ of it. What part of a quart did he use?

SUFFIXES

Each of these **suffixes** means "the action of doing" or "the state of being": -ion, -sion, -ation, and -ition.

After each word below, write its base word. Use a dictionary to check the spelling.

1. prevention _____
2. action _____
3. observation _____
4. invitation _____
5. direction _____
6. decoration _____
7. exploration _____
8. location _____
9. suggestion _____
10. introduction _____

The suffix -ment means "the action of doing," "the state of being," or "a thing that"

The suffix -ness means "the state of being"

Complete each sentence below by adding one of the suffixes on this page to the word in front of the sentence. Write the new word on the line.

settle   11. Jamestown was the first _____ in this country.

bright   12. The sudden _____ of the sun hurt my eyes.

protect   13. A porcupine has excellent natural _____.

add   14. The Bowers family just put an _____ on their house.

imagine   15. Sometimes Jackson lets his _____ run away with him.

confuse   16. The flood caused a lot of _____ in the town.

improve   17. Ron knows that his spelling needs _____.

strange   18. There was a _____ about the house that scared Ben.

collect   19. My brother has a large _____ of CDs.

admire   20. People have great _____ for President Lincoln.

MULTIPLYING FRACTIONS AND MIXED NUMBERS

Multiply. Write each answer in lowest terms.

1. $2\frac{1}{3} \times 1\frac{1}{2} =$

2. $\frac{5}{6} \times 1\frac{1}{3} =$

3. $1\frac{2}{5} \times 1\frac{1}{4} =$

4. $2\frac{1}{2} \times 4 =$

5. $3\frac{2}{3} \times 4\frac{1}{2} =$

6. $1\frac{5}{6} \times 12 =$

7. $6\frac{4}{5} \times \frac{1}{7} =$

8. $\frac{1}{3} \times 2\frac{2}{3} =$

9. $3 \times 1\frac{2}{5} =$

10. $1\frac{1}{8} \times \frac{3}{4} =$

11. $1\frac{3}{5} \times 2\frac{1}{3} =$

12. $8 \times \frac{2}{3} =$

13. Ann spent $1\frac{1}{2}$ hours at the pool on each of 5 days. How much time did she spend there in all?

14. Luis had $1\frac{1}{4}$ pints of juice. He drank $\frac{5}{6}$ of that amount. How much did he drink?

SUFFIXES

The suffix -ful means
"full of" or
"the amount that fills"

The suffix -less means
"without"

Complete the paragraph below by writing -ful or -less on each line.

Have you ever thought about being trapped in a room _____ of panthers?
What would you do if you had a house _____ of tigers? Can you imagine being
in such a hope _____ situation? If you were the fear _____ Gunter Gebel-
Williams, you'd have had no problem at all. You'd simply tell the growling but
respect _____ cats to sit down. And they would! Gunther Gebel-Williams was the
world's most famous animal trainer. He didn't work with tooth _____ old animals
that couldn't hurt him. And his cats certainly weren't play _____ little kittens, either.
Gebel-Williams trained power _____ panthers and tigers. They could have eaten
him in a big mouth _____. One care _____ mistake by Gebel-Williams could
mean pain _____ injuries or even death. He was a care _____ man, though.
And that made him success _____. To his other traits, he added a huge
cup _____ of courage. He always personally gave his cats food by the
hand _____. So Gebel-Williams got to know them. He knew them well enough to
wear a live leopard for a shawl! Gunther Gebel-Williams performed to the
end _____ applause of circus fans all over the world.

Write each word with the suffix -ful in the correct column.

"full of"		"the amount that fills"	
_____	_____	_____	_____
_____	_____	_____	_____
_____	_____	_____	

MULTIPLICATION OF MIXED NUMBERS

Multiply.

1. $2\frac{1}{2} \times 3\frac{1}{4} =$

2. $3\frac{1}{3} \times 8 =$

3. $1\frac{1}{8} \times 2\frac{2}{3} =$

4. $1\frac{1}{2} \times 2\frac{1}{5} =$

5. $6 \times 1\frac{1}{4} =$

6. $1\frac{2}{3} \times 2\frac{1}{4} =$

7. $4\frac{1}{2} \times 1\frac{1}{2} =$

8. $1\frac{1}{3} \times 18 =$

9. $3\frac{2}{5} \times 3\frac{1}{2} =$

Find the answer to each word problem. Write your answer in lowest terms.

10. Nelson bought 5 packages of ground beef for a cookout. Each weighed $1\frac{3}{5}$ kilograms. How many kilograms did he buy altogether?

11. Zara has $2\frac{3}{4}$ yards of wire. She needs $3\frac{1}{2}$ times as much wire for a project. How many yards of wire does she need?

PREFIXES AND SUFFIXES

Prefixes		**Suffixes**		
in-, im-, dis-, un-	sub-	-ion, -sion, -ation, -ition	-y, -ly	-less
pre-	inter-	-er, -or	-ment	-ist
fore-	re-	-able, -ible	-ness	-al
mis-		-ous	-ful	-ish

Complete each sentence by adding one of the prefixes above to the word below the line.

1. I find it a help to _____ my work for each coming week.
   plan

2. I will not be able to _____ you until next week.
   pay

3. Large _____ highways connect the Atlantic and Pacific coasts.
   state

4. Please do not _____ the library books.
   use

Complete each sentence by adding one of the suffixes above to the word below the line.

5. Tiana's _____ kept her home for ten days.
   ill

6. My latest _____ seems to be working.
   invent

7. The rug will not fit unless the _____ of the room is correct.
   measure

8. Fog has caused the late _____ of Jenna's plane.
   arrive

Underline the prefixes and the suffixes in the words below. Then write the base words on the lines.

9. discontinue _____

10. violinist _____

11. noticeable _____

12. juicy _____

13. subplot _____

14. painless _____

15. traveler _____

16. foresee _____

17. unaware _____

18. childish _____

19. collector _____

20. disrespectful _____

21. immovable _____

22. observation _____

PROBLEM SOLVING: MULTIPLICATION OF FRACTIONS

Find the answer to each word problem. Write your answer in lowest terms.

1. Sofia bought $\frac{1}{2}$ pound of cheese. She gave $\frac{1}{2}$ of it to Umar. How much cheese did she give to Umar?

2. Fred made 7 picnic tables. Each one took him $6\frac{1}{4}$ hours to make. How long did it take him to make all the tables?

3. The trail from the parking lot to Lacey Falls is $\frac{7}{8}$ mile long, and $\frac{2}{3}$ of that distance is uphill. What fraction of a mile is uphill?

4. How much milk does Chantal's family drink in 14 days if they drink $\frac{1}{2}$ gallon every day?

5. A beef roast weighs $3\frac{1}{3}$ pounds. It must cook $\frac{3}{4}$ hour for each pound. How long should it cook?

6. Greg sleeps $\frac{1}{3}$ of the day. There are 24 hours in a day. How many hours does Greg sleep?

7. Bret made $4\frac{1}{2}$ quarts of lemonade. His friends drank $\frac{3}{5}$ of it. How much lemonade did they drink?

8. Ayame spent $2\frac{1}{6}$ hours building a birdhouse. She spent $3\frac{1}{2}$ times as long on a doghouse. How many hours did she spend building a doghouse?

COMPREHENSION: SEQUENCE

Castle Candles

- 1 medium clay flowerpot
- an empty tin coffee can
- 1/4 pound colorless wax
- 1 or 2 crayons, any color
- 10 inches of candlewick
- a small piece of tape
- sand
- a pencil
- a large piece of newspaper
- 1 very small rock

1 First, gather everything you will need. Then ask an adult to help you. Hot wax can burn your skin. So you will want an adult to handle the hot wax.

2 Next, you will prepare the wax. Break up the wax into smaller pieces that will fit into the coffee can. Add your crayon to make the wax the color of your choice. Fill a small saucepan with a few inches with water. Then put the can into the water. Ask an adult to put the burner on low. This will melt the wax.

3 While the wax melts, make your candle mold. Lay out the newspaper over your working area. Look at the bottom of the flowerpot. If there are any holes on the bottom of your flowerpot, put tape over them. Next, fill the flowerpot with sand. Then add some water to make the sand moist enough that you can mold it. With your fingers, dig out the shape you want your castle to be. You could even press seashells, wooden blocks, or a pencil into the sand to make different shapes in it. The wax will take whatever shape that you make into the sand. Don't forget that you are making the candle upside down. So the bottom will really be the top of your castle.

4 Then you need to put in the candlewick. Cut the candlewick two inches longer than the height of the flowerpot. Tie a very small rock to the end of the candlewick. Wind the other end around a pencil. Make sure the wick is straight. Push the rock to the very bottom of the flowerpot. Balance the pencil on the top of the flowerpot. The wick has to go straight through from the bottom to the top of the candle.

5 Finally, ask an adult to pour the melted wax into the sand mold. The person should pour until the wax reaches the top of the sand mold. Let the wax cool for a day. The wax should be hard to the touch. When your wax is very hard, you can take out your candle. Turn the flowerpot upside down on a piece of newspaper. All the sand will come out. Carefully remove the candle. Take the rock off the top of your castle. And let an adult light it for you.

1. According to the directions, what is the first thing you need to do when making candles?

A Gather everything you need.

B Ask an adult to help you.

C Prepare the wax.

D Make the candle mold.

2. What should you do before you make the candle mold?

   A Prepare the wax.

   B Fill a flowerpot with sand.

   C Put in the candlewick.

   D Pour in the melted wax.

3. **Part A**

   When should you take your candle out of the mold?

   A after an hour or two

   B when the wax is hard

   C after a week

   D after a month

   Part B

   Underline the sentence in the passage that helped you find your answer to Part A.

4. When do you need to use the little rock?

   A after the wax hardens

   B while making the mold

   C while preparing the wax

   D before adding the sand

5. What is the last step in making this candle?

   _____

   _____

6. Answer the following question on a separate piece of paper.

   What do you think would happen if you forgot the step in paragraph 4? How would that affect the rest of the project?

DIVIDING WHOLE NUMBERS BY FRACTIONS

Use the pictures to help you divide.

1. $2 \div \frac{1}{2} =$

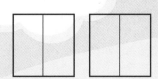

2. $3 \div \frac{1}{3} =$

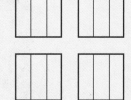

3. $4 \div \frac{1}{2} =$

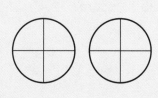

4. $3 \div \frac{1}{4} =$

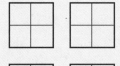

5. $4 \div \frac{1}{3} =$

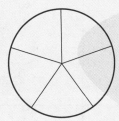

6. $2 \div \frac{1}{4} =$

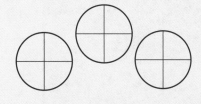

7. $4 \div \frac{1}{4} =$

8. $1 \div \frac{1}{5} =$

9. $3 \div \frac{1}{2} =$

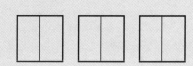

Solve.

10. A box contains 6 cups of cereal. If a serving is $\frac{1}{2}$ cup, how many servings are in the box?

11. A bag holds 8 cups of nuts. If a serving is $\frac{1}{3}$ cup, how many servings are in the bag?

PROBLEM SOLVING: FRACTIONS

Read and solve each problem. Write the answer in lowest terms.

1. On her first try, Corina jumped $6\frac{1}{12}$ feet. The second time, she jumped $7\frac{5}{12}$ feet. How much farther did she jump the second time?

2. The swim team practiced $2\frac{1}{6}$ hours on Wednesday and $4\frac{1}{2}$ hours Saturday. How many hours did the team practice this week?

3. Rafael's team scored 28 points. Rafael scored $\frac{3}{4}$ of the points. How many points did he score?

4. Satori ran 5 miles on a track today. If the track is $\frac{1}{4}$ mile long, how many times did she run around the track?

5. Darwin ran for 3 hours this week. If he ran for $\frac{1}{2}$ hour at a time, how many times did he go running?

6. A football game lasted $3\frac{1}{2}$ hours. Mai could stay only $\frac{4}{5}$ of that time. How long did she stay?

7. Clyde ran $3\frac{1}{3}$ miles on Friday. On Saturday, he ran $4\frac{2}{7}$ times that distance. How far did Clyde run on Saturday?

8. Vivian can easily lift $10\frac{1}{2}$ pounds of weights. She wants to lift $2\frac{2}{3}$ times as many pounds. How many pounds does she want to lift?

WORD USAGE

I want to _____ all about horses. My mom is
learn   teach

_____ judge at horse shows. She has promised to
a   an

_____ me how to spot a _____
learn   teach   good   well

horse. I can already ride _____. My younger
good   well

brother has _____ interest in horses, too. He
a   an

_____ ride a large horse. But he can saddle his
don't   doesn't

pony by _____.
himself   hisself

Dad has a pet shop. He will often _____ me mind
let   leave

the store when he has to _____. Dad raises hamsters.
let   leave

He has trained them to _____ up and to
sit   set

_____ down at his command. And guess
lie   lay

_____ has to take care of _____
who   whom   those   them

animals? They can open the latch on their cage by

_____. It isn't _____ fun trying to
theirself   themselves   no   any

capture _____ again!
those   them

CUSTOMARY UNITS OF LENGTH

12 inches (in.)	=	1 foot (ft)
3 feet	=	1 yard (yd)
36 inches	=	1 yard
5,280 feet	=	1 mile (mi)
1,760 yards	=	1 mile

Complete.

1. 5 feet = _____ inches

2. 4 yards = _____ feet

3. 3 yards = _____ feet

4. 2 miles = _____ feet

5. 48 inches = _____ feet

6. $\frac{1}{2}$ mile = _____ yards

7. 6 feet and 8 inches = _____ inches

8. 47 yards = _____ feet

9. 12 yards and 1 foot = _____ feet

10. 120 inches = _____ feet

11. 1 mile and 240 yards = _____ yards

12. 180 inches = _____ yards

13. 30 inches = _____ feet and _____ inches

14. 26 feet = _____ yards and _____ feet

15. 10,000 feet = _____ mile and _____ feet

Solve. Be careful. Some problems may have more than one step.

16. Harvey bought two boards to build some shelves. One is 7 feet 8 inches long, and the other is 7 feet 10 inches long. What is their total length?

17. Greta has two pieces of cloth. One piece is 3 yards 1 foot long and the other is 2 yards 2 feet long. How much cloth did Greta buy in all?

18. Mrs. Tate is 5 feet 3 inches tall. Her daughter is 4 feet 8 inches tall. How much taller is Mrs. Tate?

19. Allen bought 2 yards of ribbon. He used 2 feet 9 inches of ribbon on each of two banners. How much ribbon does he have left?

COMMA USAGE

a. A comma is used after a word like <u>yes</u>, <u>no</u>, or <u>well</u> when it is the first word of a sentence.

b. A comma is used to separate the name of a person spoken to from the rest of the sentence.

c. A comma is used to separate the day from the year in a date and the year from the rest of the sentence.

d. A comma is used to separate the name of a city from the name of a state and the name of the state from the rest of the sentence.

e. A comma is used to separate words in a series.

Place commas where they belong in the sentences below. Above each comma, write the letter of the sentence above that tells why it is needed.

1. Hannah what is Mardi Gras?

2. In New Orleans Louisiana it is a holiday.

3. This festival Juan comes at the end of a long carnival.

4. People wear purple green and gold.

5. There were balls king cakes and floats.

6. Parades costumes and banners were everywhere.

7. The first American Mardi Gras was held on March 16 1766.

8. Well is it a national holiday?

9. No it is most famous in Alabama Florida and Mississippi.

10. Actually Biloxi Mississippi and Mobile Alabama even have their own Mardi Gras.

CUSTOMARY UNITS OF CAPACITY AND WEIGHT

Complete.

2 cups (C) = 1 pint (pt)
2 pints = 1 quart (qt)
4 quarts = 1 gallon (gal)

1. $\frac{1}{2}$ gallon = _____ quarts

2. 10 gallons = _____ quarts

3. $3\frac{1}{2}$ quarts = _____ pints

4. 1 gallon = _____ pints

5. 2 quarts = _____ cups

6. 18 pints = _____ gallons and _____ quart

7. 20 cups = _____ pints or _____ quarts

Complete.

16 ounces (oz) = 1 pound (lb)
2,000 pounds = 1 ton

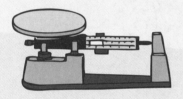

8. $\frac{1}{4}$ pound = _____ ounces

9. 8 ounces = _____ pound

10. 22 ounces = _____ pound and _____ ounces

11. $3\frac{1}{2}$ pounds = _____ ounces

12. 70 ounces = _____ pounds and _____ ounces

13. $4\frac{1}{2}$ tons = _____ pounds

14. 12,000 pounds = _____ tons

Solve. Be careful. Some problems may have more than one step.

15. Mr. Spivak had 5 gallons of gas. He used 1 gallon in his tractor and 3 quarts in his lawn mower. How much gas was left?

16. Ross sold 36 boxes of band candy. Each box weighs 12 ounces. What is the total weight in pounds of the candy Ross sold?

17. A 2-pound box of detergent sells for $4.80. A 48-ounce box sells for $5.76. Which package is the better buy?

18. A gallon jug of milk sells for $3.88. A quart sells for $1.54. How much money can Yana save by buying a gallon of milk in a gallon jug rather than by quarts?

DIRECT QUOTATIONS

Quotation marks (" ") come before and after the exact words spoken in a direct quotation. They usually come after other punctuation marks.

Joe asked, "Which famous American are you reporting on?"
"I picked George Washington Carver," said Mackenzie.

Place quotation marks where they belong in each sentence below.

1. Didn't he do something with peanuts? asked Shing.

2. Yes, he found more than 300 ways to use them, answered Mackenzie.

3. She declared, Dr. Carver made soap, printer's ink, and even a substitute for milk from peanuts!

4. Shing added, He also taught farmers to grow more crops on their land without hurting the soil.

5. I've chosen Thomas Edison for my report, Joe said.

6. Molly exclaimed, He's really famous!

7. Do you think we'd still be using oil lamps if Edison hadn't invented the light bulb? asked Mackenzie.

8. Shing said, I think someone else would probably have invented it.

9. Well, the person I'm reporting on might not be famous without Edison's help, Molly said.

10. Who is that? asked Joe.

11. Molly answered, I picked Taylor Swift.

12. She continued, If Edison hadn't invented the phonograph, we might not be able to hear her sing!

METRIC UNITS OF LENGTH

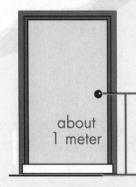

about 1 meter

The **meter** (m) is the basic metric unit for measuring length.

100 centimeters = 1 meter

The **kilometer** (km) is used for measuring long distances.

1,000 meters = 1 kilometer

Redwood

12 kilometers

CAPITAL CITY

Complete.

1. 200 centimeters = _____ meters

2. 150 centimeters = _____ meters

3. 6.5 meters = _____ centimeters

4. 5 kilometers = _____ meters

5. 1.68 meters = _____ centimeters

6. 3.25 kilometers = _____ meters

7. 3 meters = _____ centimeters

8. 8,000 meters = _____ kilometers

9. 725 centimeters = _____ meters

10. 4,500 meters = _____ kilometers

11. 2.5 kilometers = _____ meters

12. 2,650 meters = _____ kilometers

Write centimeters, meters, or kilometers to complete each sentence.

13. Ten-year-old Tony is 138 _____ tall.

14. The distance from New York City to Philadelphia is 149 _____ .

15. Lee, our basketball star, is nearly 2 _____ tall.

16. Nora swam the 300 _____ across the lake in only a few minutes.

17. That old car has been driven over 250,000 _____ .

18. I need a frame for a photograph that measures 7.6 by 12.7 _____ .

19. Victor gasped as 50 or 60 _____ of fishing line disappeared.

Solve.

20. How many 10-centimeter-long bookmarks can Yelena cut from a ribbon that is 4 meters long?

21. How many kilometers can Armando walk in an hour if he walks at the rate of 80 meters per minute?

DIRECT QUOTATIONS

Rewrite each direct quotation correctly.

1. do you see that beaver asked Brianna

   _____

   _____

2. what strong teeth it has exclaimed Kenji

   _____

   _____

3. Dion stated the teeth are curved for gnawing stumps

   _____

   _____

4. Kesha asked what is that mound

   _____

   _____

5. that is the beaver's lodge explained Eddie

   _____

   _____

6. he added it's made of chunks of wood

   _____

   _____

METRIC UNITS OF CAPACITY AND MASS

The **milliliter** (mL) and **liter** (L) are metric units of capacity.

about
1 milliliter

1,000 milliliters = 1 liter

 about
1 liter

Circle the best answer for the capacity.

1. a spoon   1 mL   1 L
2. a bucket   10 mL   10 L
3. a juice glass   10 mL   100 mL

4. a picnic cooler   4 L   40 L
5. a bathtub   10 L   100 L
6. a test tube   6 mL   6 L

Complete.

7. 2 liters = _____ milliliters
8. 3,000 milliliters = _____ liters
9. 1.5 liters = _____ milliliters

10. 5,600 milliliters = _____ liters
11. 9.8 liters = _____ milliliters
12. 500 milliliters = _____ liters

The **milligram** (mg) , **gram** (g), and **kilogram** (kg) are metric units of mass.

about
1 gram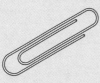

1,000 milligrams = 1 gram
1,000 grams = 1 kilogram

 about
1 kilogram

Circle the best answer for the mass of each item.

13. a bean   1 mg   1 g
14. a pair of shoes   1 g   1 kg
15. a small dog   10 kg   100 kg

16. a grain of salt   1 mg   1,000 mg
17. a football player   50 kg   100 kg
18. a slice of bread   25 g   250 g

Complete.

19. 5 kilograms = _____ grams
20. 7,000 milligrams = _____ grams
21. 1.5 kilograms = _____ grams

22. 1.8 grams = _____ milligrams
23. 3.2 kilograms = _____ grams
24. 700 grams = _____ kilogram

COMPREHENSION: INFERENCES

Read the passage. Then answer the questions.

1   Sharks have very keen senses. They use all their senses to help them hunt. Since a shark relies on so many senses, when even one sense is not working well, the shark is not able to hunt as well.

2   Many sharks can smell their food from miles away. Some can smell a single drop of blood in hundreds of gallons of water. Since most sharks have a nostril on either side of their heads, they can even tell what direction the scent is coming from.

3   Most sharks have eyes on either side of their heads, as well. This helps them to see over a wide area as they hunt for food. They also listen carefully to noises. They can hear noises that wounded animals make from far away; then they swim towards the sound.

4   Sharks use their senses of taste and touch to test if something is edible. They may nudge something or take a small bite of it. This helps them decided if they can eat it.

5   Sharks have some unusual senses that help them find prey. One of these senses is known as the lateral line. This is a row of cells along both sides of the shark's body. The water makes small movements as fish swim through it. These special cells pick up vibrations from fish or other animals as they swim through the water. Sharks can pick up vibrations that are as far as 100 feet away.

6   Another unusual sense is called the ampullae (am•PULL•ee) of Lorenzini. These are tiny fluid-filled bubbles in the shark's jaws. Using them, sharks can detect electrical signals given off by moving muscles. These signals help sharks even find creatures that have dug themselves into the sand to hide. And when a fish or person is hurt, its muscles give off extra strong electrical signals. The shark easily hones in on these signals.

1. What does the word "vibrations" mean in this passage?

    A   sounds of small movements

    B   smells of people and fish nearby

    C   bubbles from other fish and humans

    D   a row of cells on the body of a shark

2. **Part A**

What might happen if a shark's nostrils were plugged?

A It's sense of sight would get stronger to make up for it.

B It would not be able to locate food as easily.

C It would die.

D It would not be able to decide if something is edible.

Part B

Underline one or two sentences in the passage that helped you find your answer to Part A.

3. What does the phrase "hones in" mean in this passage?

A smells a scent   C loses its focus

B prepares to fight   D sharpens its focus

4. **Part A**

What happens when a fish or person is hurt in the water?

A A shark will know and probably attack.

B A shark will move to the sand to hide.

C A shark will blow bubbles to try to save them.

D A shark will swim more than 100 feet to find them.

Part B

Which of the following statements from the passage best supports your answer to Part A?

A "These special cells pick up vibrations from fish or other animals as they swim through the water."

B "These signals help sharks even find creatures that have dug themselves into the sand to hide."

C "And when a fish or person is hurt, its muscles give off extra strong electrical signals."

D "These are tiny fluid-filled bubbles in the shark's jaws."

5. Answer the following question on a separate sheet of paper.

What would probably happen if a shark found a piece of wood floating in the ocean? Explain.

CUSTOMARY MEASUREMENTS

5-Way Chili

Serves 8 people.

Sauce: $1\frac{1}{2}$ C chopped onions

$2\frac{1}{2}$ lb ground beef

one 14-oz can tomato sauce

3 C beef broth

4 T chili powder

$1\frac{1}{4}$ lb spaghetti, cooked

Toppings: 12 oz shredded cheese

one 15-oz can kidney beans

$\frac{3}{4}$ C chopped onions

Directions: 1. Brown the onions and the meat. Pour off the fat.

2. Add the tomato sauce, broth, and chili powder. Cook for 1 hour.

3. To serve "5-way," ladle sauce over spaghetti. Top with cheese, beans, and onions.

Use the information in the recipe to help you solve each problem. Check your answers.

1. Onions are used in both the sauce and as a topping. How many cups of onions does Earl need to make one recipe of chili?

2. Olivia has 3 pounds of ground beef. If she makes one recipe of chili, how many ounces of meat will she have left?

3. Naoko wants to make enough chili for 16 people. How much meat will he need?

4. How many pounds and ounces of cheese should Faith shred to make the recipe for 12 people?

5. How many quarts of broth will Clayton need to make the recipe for 32 people?

6. Robyn wants to make the recipe for only 4 people. How much meat should she use?

7. Kelsey has a 1-lb 6-oz can of kidney beans. If she uses the amount called for in the recipe, how many ounces will she have left?

8. If Jared makes one recipe, how many ounces of spaghetti would each person get if it is shared equally?

PROBLEM SOLVING: MEASUREMENT

Find the answer to each word problem.

1. Each step Doris takes is 2 feet long. How many steps will she take in 1 mile?

2. Sandor has a board that is 8 feet long. He cuts off a piece that is 54 inches long. How many inches long is the remaining piece?

3. Wayne cut 5 pieces of wire to use in a ship model. Each piece was 20 centimeters long. How many meters of wire did he use?

4. Jim has a rock with a mass of 400 grams and another with a mass of 600 grams. How many kilograms do they weigh in all?

5. A quart of paint costs $15. A gallon of the same paint costs $42. How much less does a gallon cost than the same amount in quarts?

6. Amanda mixes 10 ounces of almonds, 14 ounces of walnuts, and 24 ounces of peanuts. How many pounds of mixed nuts did she make?

7. Boris mixed 500 milliliters each of orange juice, apple juice, and soda. How many liters of punch did he make?

8. Pine Campground is 2 kilometers from the park entrance. Oakwood Campground is 750 meters from the entrance. How much closer is Oakwood than Pine to the park entrance?

ALPHABETICAL ORDER

Topics in reference volumes are listed in alphabetical order.

Number these topics in alphabetical order.

____ reindeer

____ fashion

____ earthworms

____ doves

____ beavers

____ jade

____ germs

____ breadfruit

____ valves

____ bamboo

____ snowflakes

____ lumber

Write the correct volume number to complete each sentence.

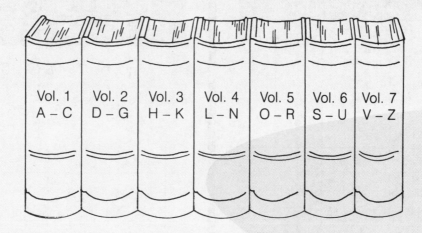

Vol. 1 A – C Vol. 2 D – G Vol. 3 H – K Vol. 4 L – N Vol. 5 O – R Vol. 6 S – U Vol. 7 V – Z

1. You would look for the topic <u>radar</u> in Vol. _____.

2. Vol. _____ would tell about <u>mammals</u>.

3. Information about <u>vision</u> would be in Vol. _____.

4. The topic <u>antiques</u> would be in Vol. _____.

5. You would find the topic <u>sailboats</u> in Vol. _____.

6. Vol. _____ would tell about <u>education</u>.

ORDERED PAIRS

Name the ordered pair for each star.

1. A _____
2. B _____
3. C _____
4. D _____
5. E _____
6. F _____
7. G _____

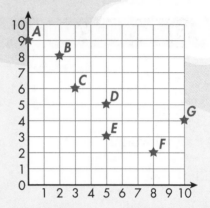

Name the point for each ordered pair.

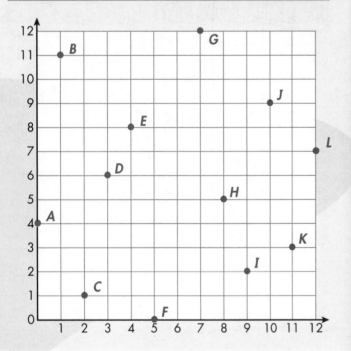

8. (12, 7) _____
9. (1, 11) _____
10. (8, 5) _____
11. (3, 6) _____
12. (10, 9) _____
13. (0, 4) _____

14. (7, 12) _____
15. (2, 1) _____
16. (11, 3) _____
17. (9, 2) _____
18. (4, 8) _____
19. (5, 0) _____

Graph and label the points below. Then draw the line segments.

A (0, 6)   B (5, 10)   C (10, 6)
D (8, 0)   E (2, 0)
$\overline{AC}$ $\overline{AD}$ $\overline{BD}$ $\overline{BE}$ $\overline{EC}$

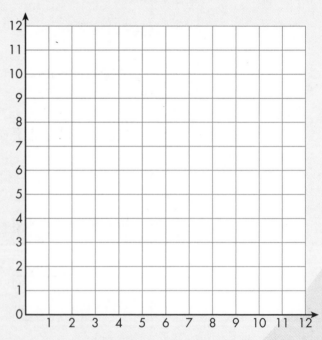

HOMOGRAPHS

Homographs are words that are spelled alike but have completely different meanings. They are listed separately in a dictionary.

Look up the following homographs in a dictionary. Write the meanings given for each one.

1. scale[1] _____

   scale[2] _____

2. ear[1] _____

   ear[2] _____

3. fan[1] _____

   fan[2] _____

4. post[1] _____

   post[2] _____

Look up each underlined word. Write the best meaning for the word as it is used in the sentence.

5. They released a <u>dove</u> at her wedding.

   _____

6. Did you see the sheep in their <u>pen</u>?

   _____

7. Please <u>hail</u> a cab for us.

   _____

8. Rowena dropped the <u>toast</u> on her lap.

   _____

9. Our <u>shed</u> is full of garden tools.

   _____

MEASURING ANGLES

Use a protractor to measure each angle. Write the measure inside the angle.

1.
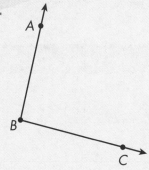

2.
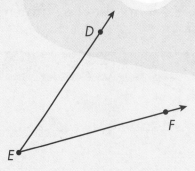

3.
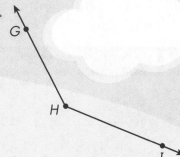

4.
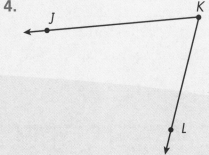

5.
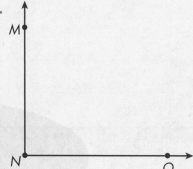

6.
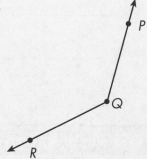

7.
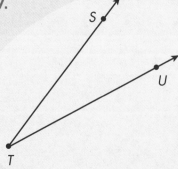

8.
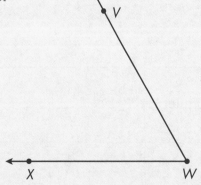

9.
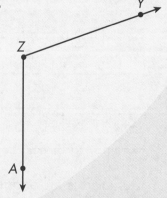

SYLLABICATION

Divide the words in each group into syllables. On the line in front of each word, write the letter of the word in the box that is divided in the same way. (Sometimes more than one letter can be used.)

---

a. Double consonants—mit | ten
b. Unlike consonants—hun | ger
c. Short vowel/consonant/vowel—rap | id
d. Long vowel/consonant/vowel—ci | der
e. Consonant before le—mar | ble
f. Between two vowels—po | et

_____ 1. habit   _____ 2. runner   _____ 3. castle

_____ 4. collect   _____ 5. dial   _____ 6. certain

_____ 7. couple   _____ 8. beaver   _____ 9. crayon

_____ 10. label   _____ 11. timber   _____ 12. lemon

_____ 13. member   _____ 14. finish   _____ 15. riot

_____ 16. heaven   _____ 17. creature   _____ 18. puzzle

_____ 19. real   _____ 20. beyond   _____ 21. cover

_____ 22. turtle   _____ 23. bacon   _____ 24. picnic

---

g. Blend or digraph—pro | gram, thick | et
h. Prefix or suffix—un | like, wood | en
i. Compound word—bull | dog

_____ 25. sunshine   _____ 26. disgrace   _____ 27. pancake

_____ 28. lonely   _____ 29. nowhere   _____ 30. orchard

_____ 31. prefix   _____ 32. mouthful   _____ 33. speechless

_____ 34. daylight   _____ 35. somehow   _____ 36. railroad

_____ 37. leafy   _____ 38. flashlight   _____ 39. eyebrow

_____ 40. redo   _____ 41. breathless   _____ 42. unload

_____ 43. twister   _____ 44. bushel   _____ 45. windshield

_____ 46. schoolroom   _____ 47. firefly   _____ 48. misspell

PERIMETER

The **perimeter** (*P*) of a figure is the distance around it.

Add to find the perimeter of each figure.

1.

4 cm 6 cm 5 cm

P = _____ cm

2.
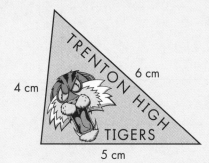

2 ft 2 ft 2 ft 2 ft 2 ft

P = _____ ft

3.
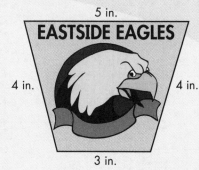

5 in. 4 in. 4 in. 3 in.

P = _____ in.

Find the perimeter of each square or rectangle.

4.

15 ft

P = _____ ft

5.

8 cm

10 cm

P = _____ cm

6.

6 yd

18 yd

P = _____ yd

7. a rectangle; *l* = 22 m, *w* = 7 m

P = _____ m

8. a square; *l* = 25 in.

P = _____ in.

9. a rectangle; *l* = 100 cm, *w* = 50 cm

P = _____ cm

10. a square; *l* = 3 in.

P = _____ in.

11. a rectangle; *l* = 9 ft, *w* = 2 ft

P = _____ ft

12. a square; *l* = 2 km

P = _____ km

DICTIONARY: SCHWA

Every dictionary includes in its pronunciation key a symbol that looks like an upside down e. This symbol is called a **schwa.** It stands for the vowel sound often heard in a syllable that is not stressed. Each vowel can have the sound of the schwa. The pronunciation key gives words to help pronounce it.

sofa	barrel	dolphin	anchor	column
sō´ fə	bar´ əl	dol´ fən	ang´ kər	kol´ əm

In each word below, circle the vowel that stands for the schwa sound.

1. upper	2. tailor	3. disease	4. bacon
5. purpose	6. temper	7. success	8. support
9. wizard	10. zebra	11. siren	12. ashore
13. council	14. perform	15. effect	16. fossil
17. doubtful	18. canyon	19. capture	20. canoe

On the line in front of each respelling, write the letter of its word.

_____ 21. plā´ ər	a. perform		_____ 31. sə lüt	k. sample
_____ 22. prə nouns	b. persuade		_____ 32. shep´ərd	l. sputter
_____ 23. pān´tər	c. partner		_____ 33. sə plī	m. shelter
_____ 24. pärt´nər	d. player		_____ 34. stub´ ərn	n. salute
_____ 25. peb´əl	e. purpose		_____ 35. sam´ pəl	o. simple
_____ 26. pər fôrm	f. pattern		_____ 36. shel´ tər	p. supply
_____ 27. pat´ ərn	g. provide		_____ 37. shuf´ əl	q. shuffle
_____ 28. pər swād	h. painter		_____ 38. sput´ ər	r. symbol
_____ 29. prə vīd	i. pronounce		_____ 39. sim´ pəl	s. stubborn
_____ 30. pėr´ pəs	j. pebble		_____ 40. sim´ bəl	t. shepherd

AREA

The **area** (A) of a figure is the number of square units inside it.

Find the area of each figure.

1.

2 cm ☐

$A =$ _____ cm^2

2.

5 ft ▭
9 ft

$A =$ _____ ft^2

3.

8 m ▯
3 m

$A =$ _____ m^2

4. a square; $l = 20$ ft

$A =$ _____ ft^2

5. a rectangle; $l = 15$ cm, $w = 10$ cm

$A =$ _____ cm^2

6. a square; $l = 9$ mi

$A =$ _____ mi^2

7.

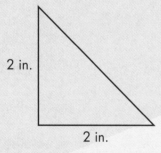

2 in.

2 in.

$A =$ _____ in.^{2}

8.

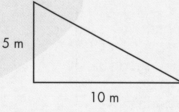

5 m

10 m

$A =$ _____ m^2

9.

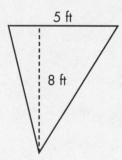

5 ft

8 ft

$A =$ _____ ft^2

10. a triangle; $b = 8$ mi, $h = 8$ mi

$A =$ _____ mi^2

11. a triangle; $b = 20$ cm, $h = 5$ cm

$A =$ _____ cm^2

12. a triangle; $b = 25$ m, $h = 10$ m

$A =$ _____ m^2

COMPREHENSION: ANALYZING LANGUAGE

from The Secret Garden

by Frances Hodgson Burnett

When her parents die, Mary Lennox is sent from India to live in her uncle's old house in Yorkshire, England. Mary hates her new home at first. Slowly she begins to enjoy it after finding a special key.

1   Mary skipped round all the gardens and round the orchard, resting every few minutes. At length she went to her own special walk and made up her mind to try to skip the whole length of it. It was a good long skip, and she began slowly, but before she had gone half-way down the path she was so hot and breathless that she was obliged to stop. She did not mind much, because she had already counted up to 30. She stopped with a little laugh of pleasure, and there, lo and behold, was the robin swaying on a long branch of ivy. He had followed her, and he greeted her with a chirp. As Mary had skipped toward him she felt something heavy in her pocket strike against her at each jump, and when she saw the robin she laughed again.

2   "You showed me where the key was yesterday," she said. "You ought to show me the door today; but I don't believe you know!"

3   The robin flew from his swinging spray of ivy on the top of the wall and he opened his beak and sang a loud, lovely trill, merely to show off. Nothing in the world is quite as adorably lovely as a robin when he shows off—and they are nearly always doing it.

4   Mary Lennox always said what happened almost at that moment was Magic.

5   One of the nice little gusts of wind rushed down the walk, and it was stronger than the rest. It was strong enough to wave the branches of the trees, and it was more than strong enough to sway the trailing sprays of untrimmed ivy hanging from the wall. Mary had stepped close to the robin, and suddenly the gust of wind swung aside some loose ivy trails, and more suddenly still she jumped toward it and caught it in her hand. This she did because she had seen something under it—a round knob which had been covered by the leaves hanging over it. It was the knob of a door.

6   She put her hands under the leaves and began to pull and push them aside. Thick as the ivy hung, it nearly all was a loose and swinging curtain, though some had crept over wood and iron. Mary's heart began to thump and her hands to shake a little in her delight and excitement. The robin kept singing and twittering away and tilting his head on one side, as if he were as excited as she was. What was this under her hands which was square and made of iron and which her fingers found a hole in?

1. The robin greeting Mary "with a chirp" is an example of which of the following?

   A   an idiom

   B   a simile

   C   personification

   D   onomatopoeia

2. In paragraph 5, "one of the nice little gusts of wind rushed down the walk." What is this an example of?

   A   foreshadowing

   B   personification

   C   a metaphor

   D   a simile

3. **Part A**

   In paragraph 6, Mary's "heart began to thump and her hands to shake a little in her delight." How was Mary feeling?

   A   angry

   B   thrilled

   C   relieved

   D   unhappy

   Part B

   Which of the following sentences from the passage best supports your answer to Part A?

   A   "She stopped with a little laugh of pleasure."

   B   "'You ought to show me the door today; but I don't believe you know!'"

   C   "The robin kept singing and twittering away and tilting his head on one side, as if he were as excited as she was."

   D   "Mary skipped round all the gardens and round the orchard, resting every few minutes."

4. Answer the following question on a separate piece of paper.

   Read this sentence from the passage.

   "Mary Lennox always said what happened almost at that moment was Magic."

   What type of figurative language is this? Explain how you know.

VOLUME

The **volume** (*V*) of a solid figure is the number of cubic units inside it.

Find the volume of each rectangular solid.

1.

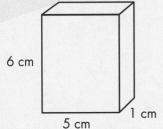

6 cm
5 cm
1 cm

$V =$ _____ cm³

2.

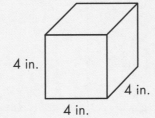

4 in.
4 in.
4 in.

$V =$ _____ in.³

3.

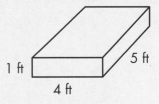

1 ft
4 ft
5 ft

$V =$ _____ ft³

4.

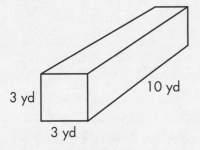

3 yd
3 yd
10 yd

$V =$ _____ yd³

5.

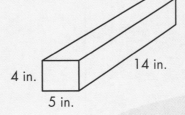

4 in.
5 in.
14 in.

$V =$ _____ in.³

6.

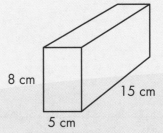

8 cm
5 cm
15 cm

$V =$ _____ cm³

7. *l* = 7 ft, *w* = 5 ft, *h* = 3 ft

$V =$ _____ ft³

8. *l* = 2 cm, *w* = 2 cm, *h* = 4 cm

$V =$ _____ cm³

9. *l* = 4 yd, *w* = 3 yd, *h* = 3 yd

$V =$ _____ yd³

10. *l* = 15 in., *w* = 5 in., *h* = 10 in.

$V =$ _____ in.³

11. *l* = 5 m, *w* = 10 m, *h* = 3 m

$V =$ _____ m³

12. *l* = 6 ft, *w* = 4 ft, *h* = 3 ft

$V =$ _____ ft³

PROBLEM SOLVING: PERIMETER, AREA, AND VOLUME

Find the answer to each word problem.

1. A picture frame is 6 inches wide and 8 inches long. What is the perimeter of this frame?

2. Nate planted potatoes in a patch 5 yards long and 3 yards wide. What is the area of the potato patch?

3. A rabbit hutch is 4 feet wide, 6 feet long, and 3 feet high. What is the volume of the rabbit hutch?

4. A tennis court is 36 feet wide and 78 feet long. What is the area of the tennis court?

5. The tennis court is inside a fenced area that is 60 feet wide and 120 feet long. What is the total length of the fence?

6. A rectangular toolbox is 8 inches wide, 20 inches long, and 10 inches high. What is the volume of the toolbox?

7. Mr. Koski marks off the area for a new garage with string. The space he marks is 24 feet wide and 30 feet long. How long is the string?

8. If Mr. Koski builds the garage to the dimensions he marked off, what will be the area the garage covers?

English Language Arts End-of-Book Review

The Basketball Game

by Yves Thibaut

1   My brother Fred made the high school basketball team. But he spent most of the season sitting on the bench. I could tell he was not happy. He's the kind of player coaches like because he tries hard and has a great attitude. But even though coaches like him, that doesn't mean they're going to let him play much in big games.

2   "You guys don't need to come to the game tonight," Fred said at breakfast one day. "It will just be a waste of time." His sigh sounded like the air leaking from a tire.

3   "I'm going anyway," I said. "You never know what will happen."

4   "Thanks, Sara," he said. "I guess it could be fun—the Wily Wolf is coming."

5   The Wily Wolf is the mascot of our city's professional basketball team. He was coming to the game to help raise money for a new library.

6   "That guy is amazing!" my dad said. "He's a true athlete. I've seen him do double back-flips, even in that bulky costume."

7   My parents and I were in the crowd at the gym that night. People were talking about the Wily Wolf. Everyone had a story about some humorous thing they had seen the mascot do. I was so excited that I didn't see the mud puddle. Sploosh! Suddenly my shoes were a mess.

8   "I'll meet you inside," I said to my parents. "I need to clean off my shoes."

9   The first restroom I came to had a line, so I walked to one at the far side of the building. There was a woman standing in the restroom holding a large plastic bag.

10   "Nice mud!" she said, laughing.

11   I laughed, too. "Thanks."

12   "I'll bet you have a brother on the team," she said. "What's his name and number?"

13   "He's Fred Davis, number 22, but he doesn't get to play much," I told her.

14   "It's great that you're here to support him," she said. "I know what it's like. I didn't get to play much on my high school team, either." She went into a stall as I wiped mud off my shoes with a paper towel. The next thing I knew, the stall door opened and the Wily Wolf emerged. My jaw dropped.

15   "Shh," she said, holding a big gloved finger up to her wolf face. I could sense a grin behind all that fur as she tiptoed out of the restroom.

16   I was bursting to tell someone. The Wily Wolf is a woman! And I'd met her! As I walked to my seat, though, I decided to keep her secret to myself. Tonight we were there for Fred. I sat down next to my parents, ready to watch the game.

1. **Part A**

The events of the story are told from the point of view of which character?

A   Sara, Fred's sister

B   Wily Wolf, the mascot

C   Fred, a basketball player

D   Mr. Davis, Fred and Sara's dad

Part B

Which sentence supports your answer in Part A?

A   "'I'll meet you inside,' I said to my parents."

B   "'Shh,' she said, holding a big, gloved finger up to her wolf face."

C   "'You guys don't need to come to the game tonight,' Fred said at breakfast one day."

D   "'That guy is amazing!' my dad said."

2. Which is the setting for the most important event in the story?

A   a kitchen

B   a restroom

C   a new library

D   a high-school classroom

3. **Part A**

In paragraph 2, the author describes Fred's sigh by using which type of figurative language?

A   a simile

B   repetition

C   alliteration

D   personification

Part B

What is an example of onomatopoeia that the author uses in the story? Write it on the line below.

_____

4. What is the most likely reason the author wrote that Sara stepped in a puddle?

    A to provide an amusing event

    B to show that she was careless

    C to point out that she was not an athlete

    D to give her a reason to go to the restroom

5. What is the Wily Wolf's big secret? Use details from the passage to explain your answer.

_____

_____

_____

_____

The World's Largest Flower

1   The world's largest flower is the rafflesia, or flower lotus. It is 36 inches wide and weighs 15 pounds. Some rafflesias grow to 42 inches, as tall as a 5-year-old child.

2   This enormous flower is very rare. It only grows in rain forests on the islands of Sumatra and Borneo. The flower lotus has no roots, or green leaves. It is a parasite, a plant that lives off another plant.

3   The flower lotus needs wild grapevines in order to live. Squirrels and other animals chew on grapevines for food, which cuts open the vine. Insects carry the sticky flower lotus seeds on their bodies. When the insects land on an opened vine, the seeds stick to the plant. The growing seed becomes part of the grapevine, taking food from it. The grapevine doesn't seem to mind sharing with the flower lotus. A year and a half later, a flower lotus pod pushes through the surface of the vine. The bud is only two inches wide and looks like a tiny cabbage. The bud grows for nine more months before it blooms.

4   The flower lotus has five bright red leathery petals covered with raised yellow dots. Stiff spikes protect the seeds in the flower's center. This brilliant blossom only lives for four days. Then the colorful petals curl up and turn black. In a few weeks, all that is left is a slimy black mass that looks and smells like a dead animal. The smell attracts many flies and other insects, and they carry the seeds to another waiting grapevine. The cycle begins again.

6. What happens after the lotus blossom dies and becomes smelly?

   A The petals curl up.

   B Insects are drawn to the slimy mass.

   C The petals turn black.

   D Seeds form in the flower's center.

7. Which of the following does the flower lotus not have?

   A leaves

   B blossoms

   C petals

   D buds

8. What must happen so that the lotus seeds can stick to the grapevine?

   A The vine must grow a new covering.

   B The lotus bud must grow for nine months.

   C The vine must be cut open by animals.

   D The flower must grow to be 42 inches tall.

9. Which sentence best shows that the flower lotus is a parasite?

   A The flower lotus is large and beautiful.

   B The flower lotus seed takes food from the grapevine.

   C The flower lotus grows in rain forests.

   D The flower lotus blossom lasts for only four days.

10. What is this passage mostly about?

    A the life cycle of the flower lotus

    B the problems caused by the flower lotus

    C protecting plants and animals of the rain forest

    D living on the islands of Sumatra and Borneo

11. What must happen before the insects carry the seeds to the grapevine?

   _____

   _____

Note: When you hear the word "highway" today, you usually picture a wide road for automobiles and trucks. But if you go back 100 years or more, a highway was a different kind of road.

Windy Nights

by Robert Louis Stevenson

Whenever the moon and stars are set,
Whenever the wind is high,
All night long in the dark and wet
A man goes riding by,
5 Late in the night when the fires are out,
Why does he gallop and gallop about?

Whenever the trees are crying aloud
And ships are tossed at sea,
By, on the highway, low and loud,
10 By at the gallop goes he
By at the gallop he goes, and then
By he comes back at the gallop again.

12. Who is the speaker in this poem?

   A a rider

   B a horse

   C an observer

   D a ship's captain

13. **Part A**

How is the night described in the poem?

A dry

B rainy

C mild

D warm

Part B

Which line from the poem supports the answer in Part A?

A "Whenever the moon and stars are set,"

B "Whenever the wind is high,"

C "All night long in the dark and wet"

D "Late in the night when the fires are out,"

14. Which word does the poet use to rhyme with the last word in line 10?

A sea

B by

C trees

D loud

15. Read this line from the poem.

"Whenever the trees cry aloud"

What type of figurative language does the poet use in this line?

A alliteration

B repetition

C onomatopoeia

D personification

16. What is the effect of the poet's use of repetition and rhythm in the last stanza?

_____

_____

1   At a fair or carnival, you can't miss the Ferris wheel, especially at night when it's all lit up. The first Ferris wheel was a "monster." It was built in 1893 for a world's fair in Chicago. The Ferris wheel was 264 feet high and could carry more than 2,100 riders at a time. Each of its 36 cars held 60 people.

2   The first Ferris wheel was built by George Washington Ferris. Why did Ferris build such a giant ride? A few years earlier, Alexander Eiffel of Paris, France, built the Eiffel Tower, which is made of iron and stands 984 feet high. At the time, it was the tallest structure in the world and brought a lot of attention to France. Ferris thought that if he were to build the biggest ride in the world, it would bring a lot of attention to the United States.

3   The Ferris wheel did that, and more. Thousands of people waited in line to ride on it. But the problem with the Ferris wheel was that it was too big. Because of its size, it was too costly to run. And moving it was a very expensive nightmare. After the fair in Chicago closed, it took three months to take the Ferris wheel apart. The last time it was used was in 1904. The Ferris wheel was a popular ride at the St. Louis World's Fair. But it made hardly any money. Its owners decided to blow it up.

4   About a million and a half people rode on the first Ferris wheel. One of those riders was W. E. Sullivan, who built bridges for a living. He enjoyed his ride so much that he decided to go into business making Ferris wheels. He called his company the Eli Bridge Company—even though he built Ferris wheels. Sullivan figured that if he didn't make any money on them, he'd go back to building bridges. Sullivan's Ferris wheels were much smaller than the original. The first one was 45 feet high. This made them cheaper to build. They could also be moved from place to place fairly easily. That way, they could be taken to county fairs. The company Sullivan started has been building Ferris wheels ever since. And the Ferris wheel is still one of the most popular rides at fairs and carnivals.

17. What is this passage mostly about?

    A W. E. Sullivan

    B George Ferris

    C the history of the Ferris wheel

    D the Chicago World's Fair

18. How was W. E. Sullivan's Ferris wheel different than the one built by George Ferris?

    A It was made in Paris.

    B It was made of iron.

    C It was 45 feet high.

    D It had 36 cars.

19. Why was the first Ferris wheel blown up?

    A Most people were afraid to ride it.

    B It cost too much to run it.

    C It was getting old.

    D The rides took too long.

20. How were the Eiffel Tower and the Ferris wheel alike?

_____

_____

_____

_____

Writing End-of-Book Review

Read the writing prompt below.
Then plan, write, and proofread your answer.
Plan what you are going to write in the space below.
Then write your final answer on another piece of paper.

Think about something you learned in school. It could be something from history, geography, science, or any school subject. Tell readers about what you have learned.

Be sure to include details and write clearly so your readers will understand the information you are giving them.

Math End-of-Book Review

1. A deck projecting off the end of a house has the shape shown below.

   What is the perimeter of the deck?

   A   48 feet

   B   54 feet

   C   68 feet

   D   72 feet

2. Jens needs to find the sum of $\frac{2}{5}$ and $\frac{7}{15}$.

   Circle the correct choice in each set to make the following statement true.

   Since $\frac{2}{5}$ is equivalent to [$\frac{4}{10}$, $\frac{6}{10}$, $\frac{4}{15}$, $\frac{6}{15}$], the sum is [$\frac{11}{15}$, $\frac{13}{15}$, $\frac{11}{25}$, $\frac{13}{25}$, $\frac{13}{30}$].

3. Celia uses $1\frac{5}{6}$ foot of string to make a necklace. She has a spool containing enough string to make $14\frac{3}{4}$ necklaces.

   How much string is on the spool?

   _____ feet

4. Colin is 4 feet 9 inches tall. When he stands on a ladder, his height increases another 1 foot 6 inches. The ceiling is 7 feet 8 inches high.

How many inches of space are between the ceiling and Colin when he stands on the ladder?

    A 13 inches

    B 15 inches

    C 17 inches

    D 20 inches

5. Add:

$$\begin{array}{r} 15.067 \\ +\ 8.64 \\ \hline \end{array}$$

6. Look at the coordinate plane below.

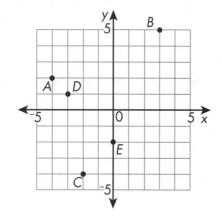

What are the coordinates for the points on this plane?

Point A _____

Point B _____

Point C _____

Point D _____

Point E _____

7. A recipe for bread dough calls for $2\frac{3}{4}$ cups of flour. Cleo plans to double this recipe. She has a package containing 8 cups of flour. How many cups will be left after Cleo makes the double recipe?

    A $2\frac{1}{4}$ cups

    B $2\frac{1}{2}$ cups

    C $5\frac{1}{4}$ cups

    D $5\frac{1}{2}$ cups

8. Use your centimeter ruler and protractor to solve this problem.
Glynnis will use the shape below as a pattern for a quilt piece.

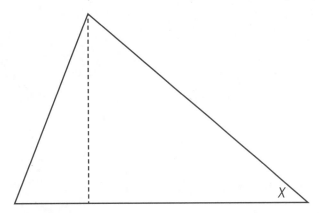

What is the area of this quilt piece pattern?

_____ square centimeters

What is the measure of the angle marked X?

_____ degrees

9. Blake bought a package of 24 trading cards. Four of the cards were already in his collection.

What fraction describes the part of the 24 cards that were already in his collection? Select all that apply.

   A $\frac{1}{8}$

   B $\frac{1}{6}$

   C $\frac{2}{12}$

   D $\frac{2}{16}$

   E $\frac{20}{24}$

   F $\frac{5}{6}$

   G $\frac{7}{8}$

10. Find the quotient.

$$14.28 \div 3 = \boxed{}$$

11. Nora weighted an apple and a peach. The apple weighed $\frac{9}{16}$ pound and the peach weighed $\frac{1}{4}$ pound.

How much heavier was the apple than the peach?

   A $\frac{5}{16}$ pound

   B $\frac{8}{16}$ pound

   C $\frac{8}{12}$ pound

   D $\frac{13}{16}$ pound

12. A bulk food store has 30 pounds of baking soda. An employee fills bags with $\frac{3}{4}$ pound of baking soda each.

How many bags can the employee fill?

_____ bags

13. A certain street is 2.5 kilometers long.

How many meters long is this street?

_____ meters

How many centimeters long is this street?

_____ centimeters

14. Trevor bought 6 bags of cat food. Each bag weighed 3.25 pounds. When he got home, he divided the food evenly into 2 storage containers.

How many pounds of food are in each container?

_____ pounds

15. Look at this jewelry box.

4 in.
10 in.   7 in.

What is the volume of this jewelry box?

_____ cubic inches

When empty, the jewelry box weighs $1\frac{1}{2}$ pounds. How many ounces does the empty jewelry box weigh?

_____ ounces

16. Jeremy bought the following amounts of cheese at the deli.

- $1\frac{3}{4}$ pounds of American cheese
- $\frac{7}{8}$ pounds of Swiss cheese
- $2\frac{1}{4}$ pounds of Munster cheese
- $\frac{1}{2}$ pound cheddar cheese

Which of the following statements is true? Select all that apply.

A   Jeremy bought $1\frac{3}{8}$ pounds more Munster cheese than Swiss cheese.

B   Jeremy bought a total of $2\frac{5}{8}$ pounds of American and Swiss cheeses.

C   Jeremy bought a total of $2\frac{3}{8}$ pounds of Munster and cheddar cheeses.

D   Jeremy bought $1\frac{1}{4}$ pounds more American cheese than cheddar cheese.

E   Jeremy bought a total of $3\frac{19}{32}$ pounds of cheese.

F   Jeremy bought a total of $5\frac{1}{2}$ pounds of cheese.

17. Antonio weighs 37 kilograms. His older sister weighs 45 kilograms. How many more grams does Antonio's sister weigh than Antonio?

_____ grams

18. A florist is using ribbon to decorate some wreaths. She uses 32 inches of ribbon per wreath. She has a roll of 800 inches of ribbon.

How many wreaths can the florist decorate with this roll of ribbon?

_____ wreaths

The florist uses 1.45 feet of ribbon in some flower arrangements. How much ribbon will she need to do 18 of these arrangements?

_____ feet

Glossary

Adjective	a word that tells about people, animals, and things
Adverb	a word that tells something about a verb
Base Word	the word that a prefix or suffix is added to
Contraction	two words written together as one word with one or more letters replaced by an apostrophe
Details	facts or information about a topic
Fragment	a group of words that is not a complete sentence
Homographs	words that are spelled the same but have different meanings
Homophones	words that sound the same but have different meanings and spellings
Main Idea	the most important idea of a story
Noun	a word that names a person, place, or thing
Possessive	the form of a word that shows ownership
Predicate	the part of a sentence that tells something about the subject
Prefix	a word part added to the beginning of a word that changes the meaning of the word
Object Pronoun	a word used in place of a noun as the object of a sentence: me, you, him, her, it
Run-On Sentence	a sentence that should be divided into two or more separate sentences
Schwa	a symbol used in a dictionary that stands for a vowel sound usually heard in a syllable that is not stressed; looks like an upside down e
Sentence	a group of words that gives a complete thought
Sequence	the order in which things happen

Subject	what a sentence is about
Subject Pronoun	a word used in place of a noun as the subject of a sentence: I, you, he, she, it
Suffix	a word part added to the end of a word that changes the meaning of the word
Syllable	a part of a word that has one vowel sound
Verb	a word that tells what people, animals, or things do

Cut-Out Math Tools

Protractor

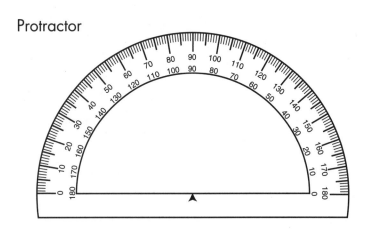

Ruler

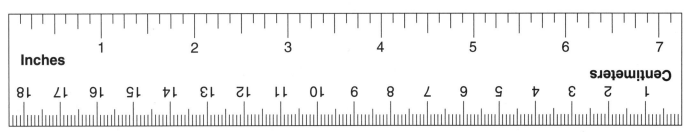

Protractor

Ruler

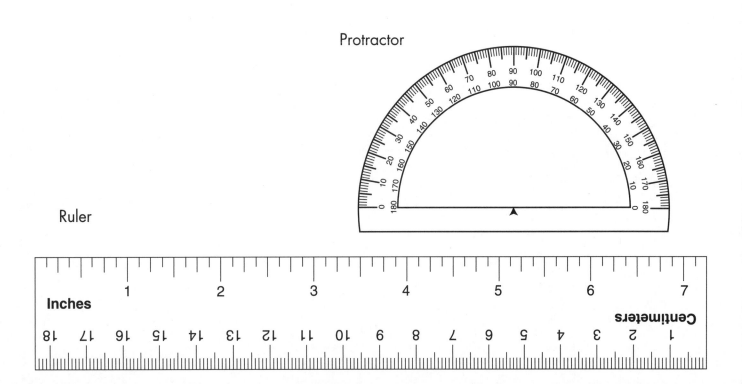

Congratulations!

_____

Name

.... has been awarded a ....

Certificate of Achievement

.... for work on ....

Continental's

Jump Start

_____

Teacher

_____

Date

Answer Key

Items in the Midpoint and End-of-Book Reviews are aligned to the Common Core State Standards. Find the full text of the CCSS at www.corestandards.org.

Week 1

Page 5: NOUNS

1. architect
2. diamond
3. melody
4. ostrich
5. acre
6. assembly
7. pilot
8. horizon
9. inspector
10. biography
11. ingredient
12. boulder
13. telephone
14. construction

Page 6: MULTIPLYING WITH MULTIPLES OF TEN

1. 21, 10, 210
   3, 70, 210
2. 45, 10, 450
   5, 90, 450
3. 42; 100; 4,200
   7; 600; 4,200

4. 60	**5.** 120	**6.** 180	**7.** 240	**8.** 300
9. 360	**10.** 240	**11.** 150	**12.** 120	**13.** 400
14. 300	**15.** 600	**16.** 900	**17.** 1,200	**18.** 1,500
19. 800	**20.** 3,600	**21.** 3,500	**22.** 5,600	**23.** 3,600

24. 650 miles per hour   25. 1,200 people

Page 7: POSSESSIVE FORM NOUNS

1. drivers'
2. coyote's
3. men's
4. Artists'
5. sheep's
6. players'
7. dancer's
8. principal's
9. children's

Page 8: MULTIPLYING NUMBERS

1. 96	**2.** 282	**3.** 255	**4.** 60	**5.** 234	**6.** 576
7. 528	**8.** 1,708	**9.** 2,812	**10.** 648	**11.** 1,944	
12. 1,995	**13.** 2,562	**14.** 592	**15.** 5,824	**16.** 8,649	
17. 27,945	**18.** 36,309	**19.** 38,410			
20. 23,337	**21.** 48,468				

22. 20,092	**23.** 129,600	**24.** 55,254	**25.** 194,570

26. $1.95	**27.** $10.71	**28.** $2.28
29. $616.50	**30.** $1,544.28	**31.** $999.92

Page 9: PRONOUN USAGE

us, We, She, her
them, They
I, them, I, him, He, me, we

Page 10: TWO-DIGIT MULTIPLICATION

1. 90
   1,350
   1,440; 90; 1,350
2. 5,592
   46,600
   52,192; 5,592; 46,600

3. 1,430	**4.** 3,182	**5.** 3,230	**6.** 2,392
7. 9,072	**8.** 6,948	**9.** 14,152	**10.** 13,110
11. 912	**12.** 144,908	**13.** 284,088	**14.** 2,590

15. $768   16. $3,750

Page 11: POSSESSIVE PRONOUNS

its, its, their
his, our
their, her, his
your, My, your, our

Page 12: THREE-DIGIT MULTIPLICATION

1. 143,724	**2.** 155,078	**3.** 327,840
4. 260,975	**5.** 476,194	
6. 290,160	**7.** 458,250	**8.** 213,597
9. 83,556	**10.** 492,954	
11. $1,597.50	**12.** $7,787.50	
13. $3,207.60	**14.** $9,012.44	

Pages 13–14: COMPREHENSION: MAIN IDEA AND DETAILS

1. C
2. A
3. C
4. D
5. *Sample answer:* Highland-Terrapin was the strongest character. He told the mama Opossum that he would rescue her babies. He followed through and rescued them even though he was hurt in the process. He had to walk across hot ash to get to the babies. Bat also tried to stop Highland-Terrapin by jumping on him. Highland-Terrapin did not let any of this stop him from rescuing the babies.

Page 15: THREE-DIGIT MULTIPLICATION
1. 190,372   **2.** 101,760   **3.** 284,811   **4.** 243,552
5. 55,279   **6.** 129,996   **7.** 289,224   **8.** 449,020
9. 410,712   **10.** 51,150   **11.** 653,660   **12.** 255,817

13. 42,550 bushels   **14.** 35,112 pounds

Page 16: PROBLEM SOLVING: TWO- AND THREE-DIGIT MULTIPLICATION
1. 6,720 miles   **2.** 19,110 words
3. 5,760 kilobytes   **4.** 9,600 calories
5. 77,440 yards   **6.** 30,752 seats
7. $112,530   **8.** 35,872 pepper plants

Week 2

Page 17: s-FORM VERBS
1. volunteers   **2.** sketches
3. watches   **4.** exists
5. envies   **6.** identifies
7. relaxes   **8.** flatters
9. mashes   **10.** magnifies
11. supplies   **12.** publishes
13. establishes   **14.** intends

Page 18: ONE-DIGIT DIVISION
1. 30   **2.** 80   **3.** 31   **4.** 74
5. 46   **6.** 32   **7.** 23   **8.** 62
9. 96 R2   **10.** 66   **11.** 44   **12.** 29 R4
13. 92   **14.** 46 R1   **15.** 32   **16.** 19

17. 49 groups   **18.** 54 hours

Page 19: PAST VERB FORMS
left, went, saw, took
said, found
had, thought, told, got, wrote
grew, came, made, did

Page 20: DIVIDING BY TWO-DIGIT NUMBERS
1. 22 R26   **2.** 23   **3.** 31 R1   **4.** 13
5. 45 R5   **6.** 28   **7.** 70 R55   **8.** 67
9. 75 R8   **10.** 39 R14   **11.** 89   **12.** 18
13. 49   **14.** 88 R12
15. 83 bags   **16.** 94 boxes

Page 21: IRREGULAR VERB FORMS
spoken, written, took, driven, ridden
flew, knew, went, grown, begun
eaten, saw, blown, hid

Page 22: DIVIDING BY TWO-DIGIT NUMBERS
1. 140 R24   **2.** 236 R1   **3.** 107
4. 152 R2   **5.** 645 R3   **6.** 963
7. 908   **8.** 247
9. 570   **10.** 218

Page 23: ADJECTIVES
1. This fresh bread has a good taste.
2. The young horses had thin legs.
3. The heavy basket was full of fresh fruit.
4. This small pencil needs a sharp point.
5. The creative boy drew a comical picture.
6. The large group climbed the tall mountain.
7. The pretty necklace is made of glass beads.

Page 24: DIVISION WITH MULTIPLES OF TEN
1. 4, 40, 400   **2.** 8, 80, 800   **3.** 6, 60, 600
4. 6, 60, 600   **5.** 7, 70, 700   **6.** 6, 60, 600
7. 7, 70, 700   **8.** 6, 60, 600   **9.** 5, 50, 500
10. 7   **11.** 3   **12.** 4   **13.** 8
14. 40   **15.** 30   **16.** 50   **17.** 40
18. 30   **19.** 40   **20.** 40   **21.** 70
22. 500   **23.** 300   **24.** 900   **25.** 300

Pages 25–26: COMPREHENSION: CAUSE AND EFFECT
1A. A
1B. *Students should have underlined,* "Then there wouldn't be enough food for them and the new foals born each spring."
2. B
3. B
4. D
5. *Sample answer:* The volunteer firefighters hold the auction to raise money for Chincoteague's fire department. The horses sell for $1,000 to $4,000 each, so this is a good fundraiser. They also do it to manage the horse population on Assateague and make sure the ponies living there will have enough to eat.

Page 27: TWO-DIGIT DIVISION
1. 30 R4   **2.** 27 R4   **3.** 12 R2
4. 31   **5.** 522 R21   **6.** 43 R24
7. 52 R2   **8.** 317 R51   **9.** 61
10. 35   **11.** 365 R10   **12.** 102

13. 15 sacks   **14.** 71 times

Page 28: PROBLEM SOLVING: TWO-DIGIT DIVISION
1. 15 cookies   **2.** 25 days
3. 24 hours   **4.** $46
5. 13 days   **6.** 39 bags, 5 potatoes left
7. 22 months   **8.** 35 rows, 10 chairs left

Week 3

Page 29: COMPARING WITH ADJECTIVES

1. slimmer, slimmest
2. more valuable, most valuable
3. dimmer, dimmest
4. riskier, riskiest
5. more honest, most honest
6. wider, widest
7. more polite, most polite
8. warmer, warmest
9. bigger, biggest
10. sillier, silliest
11. sadder, saddest
12. tastier, tastiest
13. more pleasant, most pleasant

Page 30: PLACE VALUE: LARGE NUMBERS

1. 16,457
2. 34,165
3. 70,913
4. 18,500
5. 951,987
6. 406,090
7. 80,523
8. 32,162
9. 17,040
10. 519,615
11. 400,212

12. 20,000 + 7,000 + 900 + 10 + 6
13. 80,000 + 5,000 + 800 + 70 + 5
14. 70,000 + 2,000
15. 300,000 + 90,000 + 4,000
16. 500,000 + 10,000 + 80 + 1
17. 100,000 + 90,000 + 3,000 + 500 + 60 + 7

18. 6,000
19. 50,000
20. 30
21. 0
22. 90,000
23. 4,000
24. 800,000
25. 60,000
26. 70,000
27. 0

Page 31: ADVERBS

1. here
2. away
3. tomorrow
4. well
5. yesterday
6. already
7. again
8. always
9. today
10. there

Page 32: ROUNDING LARGE NUMBERS

1. 70
2. 50
5. 360
6. 930
9. 2,020
10. 5,200

3. 30
4. 30
7. 410
8. 890
11. 1,990
12. 7,100

13. 200
14. 400
15. 300
16. 300
17. 500
18. 800
19. 1,500
20. 4,900
21. 3,200
22. 2,700
23. 8,100
24. 7,000

25. 2,000
26. 2,000
27. 8,000
28. 5,000
29. 7,000
30. 19,000
31. 24,000
32. 106,000
33. 586,000

34. 7,800
    8,000
35. 2,500
    2,000

Page 33: USING ADJECTIVES AND ADVERBS

1. adj.
2. adv.
3. adj.
4. adj.
5. adv.
6. adv.
7. adj.
8. adv.
9. adj.
10. adv.
11. adv.
12. adj.
13. adj.
14. adj.

Page 34: COMPARING AND ORDERING NUMBERS

1. <
2. >
3. <
4. >
5. >
6. <
7. <
8. >
9. >
10. >
11. >
12. >

13. 29,035 > 22,834
14. 7,310 < 16,066
15. 18,510 < 19,340
16. 22,834 > 20,320

Everest
Aconcagua
McKinley
Kilimanjaro
Elbrus
Vinson
Kosciusko

Page 35: COMPOUND WORDS

Compound words in items 1–9 may be listed in any order.

1. goldfish
2. windshield
3. airport
4. drugstore
5. somehow
6. lighthouse
7. headquarters

8. seashore
9. railroad

10. make up, make-up
11. side walk, sidewalk
12. home runs, home runs
13. left handed, left-handed
14. baby sits, baby-sits
15. funny bone, funny bone
16. frame work, framework
17. high tide, high tide
18. sun shine, sunshine
19. earth quakes, earthquakes
20. bunk beds, bunk beds

Page 36: PRIME AND COMPOSITE NUMBERS

1. 1, 2, 4; composite
2. 1, 5; prime
3. 1, 2, 3, 6; composite
4. 1, 2, 4, 8; composite
5. 1, 2, 5, 10; composite
6. 1, 11; prime
7. 1, 13; prime
8. 1, 3, 5, 15; composite

9. 2, 2, 3   10. 5, 2, 5   11. 9, 3, 3   12. 3, 3, 5

Pages 37–38: COMPREHENSION: ANALYZING LANGUAGE

1. B
2. D
3A. A
3B. *Students should have underlined the lines,* "Couched in his kennel, like a log,/With paws of silver sleeps the dog."
4. *Sample answer:* The silver light from the moon makes everything in the poem appear silver.
5. *Sample answer:* The poet is emphasizing the silver color that the moon makes. He wants the reader to keep the color of silver in his mind, so that he is really visualizing the color in everything in the poem. It also makes the moonlight seem more magical to picture everything coated in silver.

Page 39: FACTORS

1. 1 × 12, 2 × 6, 3 × 4; 1, 2, 3, 4, 6, 12
2. 1 × 5; 1, 5
3. 1 × 6, 2 × 3; 1, 2, 3, 6
4. 1 × 8, 2 × 4; 1, 2, 4, 8
5. 1 × 10; 2 × 5; 1, 2, 5, 10
6. 1 × 15, 3 × 5; 1, 3, 5, 15
7. 1 × 18, 2 × 9, 3 × 6; 1, 2, 3, 6, 9, 18
8. 1 × 20, 2 × 10, 4 × 5; 1, 2, 4, 5, 10, 20
9. 1 × 24, 2 × 12, 3 × 8, 4 × 6; 1, 2, 3, 4, 6, 8, 12, 24
10. 1 × 30, 2 × 15, 3 × 10, 5 × 6; 1, 2, 3, 5, 6, 10, 15, 30
11. 1 × 32, 2 × 16, 4 × 8; 1, 2, 4, 8, 16, 32
12. 1 × 36, 2 × 18, 3 × 12, 4 × 9, 6 × 6; 1, 2, 3, 4, 6, 9, 12, 18, 36
13. 1 × 40, 2 × 20, 4 × 10, 5 × 8; 1, 2, 4, 5, 8, 10, 20, 40
14. 1 × 45, 5 × 9; 1, 5, 9, 45
15. 1 × 48, 2 × 24, 3 × 16, 4 × 12, 6 × 8; 1, 2, 3, 4, 6, 8, 12, 16, 24, 48

16. 1 × 54, 2 × 27, 3 × 18, 6 × 9; 1, 2, 3, 6, 9, 18, 27, 54

17. 1, ⑤
18. 1, ⑤
19. 1, 2, 3, ⑥
20. 1, 2, 4, ⑧
21. 1, ⑤
22. 1, ⑤
23. 1, 2, 3, 4, 6, ⑫
24. 1, 2, 4, ⑧
25. 1, 2, 3, 6, 9, ⑱
26. 1, 2, 3, ⑥

Page 40: MULTIPLES

1. 3, 6, 9, 12, 15, 18, 21, 24, 27, 30
2. 2, 4, 6, 8, 10, 12, 14, 16, 18, 20
3. 4, 8, 12, 16, 20, 24, 28, 32, 36, 40
4. 5, 10, 15, 20, 25, 30, 35, 40, 45, 50
5. 6, 12, 18, 24, 30, 36, 42, 48, 54, 60
6. 7, 14, 21, 28, 35, 42, 49, 56, 63, 70
7. 8, 16, 24, 32, 40, 48, 56, 64, 72, 80
8. 9, 18, 27, 36, 45, 54, 63, 72, 81, 90
9. 10, 20, 30, 40, 50, 60, 70, 80, 90, 100
10. 12, 24, 36, 48, 60, 72, 84, 96, 108, 120
11. 15, 30, 45, 60, 75, 90, 105, 120, 135, 150
12. 20, 40, 60, 80, 100, 120, 140, 160, 180, 200
13. 30, 60, 90, 120, 150, 180, 210, 240, 270, 300
14. 50, 100, 150, 200, 250, 300, 350, 400, 450, 500
15. 100, 200, 300, 400, 500, 600, 700, 800, 900, 1,000
16. 1,000; 2,000; 3,000; 4,000; 5,000; 6,000; 7,000; 8,000; 9,000; 10,000

17. ⑫ 24
18. ⑮ 30
19. ⑩ 20
20. ⑳ 40
21. ⑫ 24, 36
22. ⑧ 16, 24, 32, 40
23. ⑱ 36, 54
24. ㉚ 60, 90
25. �60 120
26. ⑩⓪ 200, 300, 400, 500

Week 4

Page 41: CAPITALIZATION

1. I just read a book called The Living White House.
2. It tells about people who have lived in the White House in Washington, DC.
3. President Harrison's grandson lived there with a pet goat named His Whiskers.
4. Tad Lincoln kept a pet turkey that someone had sent his family for Christmas dinner.
5. The book also tells about the egg-roll that is held on Easter Monday at the White House.
6. Theodore Roosevelt's children had a pony named Fidelity.
7. Tricia Nixon was married in the Rose Garden at the White House.

Page 42: DECIMALS: PLACE VALUE

1. 0.3
2. 0.29
3. 9.102
4. 7.45
5. 0.074
6. 35.09
7. 0.38
8. 0.982
9. 28.008
10. 4.99
11. 0.406
12. 100.1

13. 8.2
14. 0.5
15. 1.73
16. 0.26
17. 2.205
18. 47.006

19. 0.17   **20.** 8.052
21. 400.2
22. 0.621
23. 19.04
24. 180.123

Page 43: FORMING SENTENCES

1. Students   **2.** Wounds
3. Monkeys   **4.** Lights
5. Kites   **6.** Mice
7. Spiders   **8.** Steaks

9. rattle   **10.** burst
11. squeal   **12.** whistle
13. screech   **14.** blare
15. block   **16.** crumble

Page 44: COMPARING DECIMALS

1. >   **2.** <   **3.** >
4. <   **5.** =   **6.** >
7. <   **8.** >   **9.** <
10. <   **11.** >   **12.** >
13. >   **14.** >   **15.** =
16. <   **17.** <   **18.** >

19. 0.3, 0.4, 0.9
20. 0.05, 0.32, 1.01
21. 1.96, 2.03, 3.4

22. 0.6, 0.5, 0.1
23. 0.92, 0.29, 0.2
24. 4.09, 1.78, 0.56

25. 0.2 > 0.09   **26.** 2.3 > 2.15
peanuts   2.15 kilometers

Page 45: SUBJECT AND PREDICATE

     <u>Bicycles</u> were invented in the late 1700s. <u>Two-wheelers</u> came in many shapes and sizes for the next 90 years.
     <u>The first bicycle</u> was called a walk-along. <u>The walk-along</u> had no pedals. <u>The rider</u> sat on it and pushed it with his or her feet.
     <u>The boneshaker</u> appeared in the 1860s. <u>Its wooden wheels</u> gave riders a bumpy trip. <u>The front wheel of this bicycle</u> was slightly larger than the back wheel.
     <u>The high wheeler</u> was one of the strangest bikes of all. <u>Its front wheel</u> measured 40–48 inches high. <u>The back wheel</u> was very small, however.
     <u>These early bicycles</u> were funny to look at. <u>They</u> were also very hard to ride.

Page 46: ADDING DECIMALS

1. 26.00   **2.** 0.72   **3.** 0.310   **4.** 12.5
5. 58.72   **6.** 308.8   **7.** 9.663   **8.** 77.82
9. 986.34   **10.** 670.79   **11.** 86.013   **12.** 57.058
13. 48.32   **14.** 739.6   **15.** 14.432   **16.** 118.955

17. 1.681 kilometers   **18.** 32.5 centimeters
19. 33.61 kilograms   **20.** 8.32 kilometers per hour

Page 47: END PUNCTUATION

1. S; .
2. C; .
3. S; .
4. Q; ?
5. E; !
6. S; .
7. E; !
8. Q; ?
9. C; .
10. Q; ?
11. C; .
12. E; !

Page 48: SUBTRACTING DECIMALS

1. 3.23   **2.** 4.7   **3.** 0.46   **4.** 0.178
5. 109.4   **6.** 1.949   **7.** 38.9   **8.** 2.198
9. 98.98   **10.** 0.859   **11.** 16.958   **12.** 63.576
13. 1.666   **14.** 199.99   **15.** 19.69   **16.** 79.855

17. 5.06 miles
18. 2.5 pounds
19. 32.9°   **20.** 0.007 ounce

Pages 49–50: COMPREHENSION: COMPARE AND CONTRAST

1. D
2A. *Sample answer:* Beethoven did not follow the normal musical rules.
2B. *Students should have underlined the sentence,* "While Mozart wrote his music using the same format that most composers had used, Beethoven tried to write music that did not follow the rules."
3. B
4. A
5. *Answers will vary; students should compare and contrast their favorite musical artist with either Mozart or Beethoven.*

Page 51: ADDING AND SUBTRACTING DECIMALS

1. 71.03   **2.** 48.81   **3.** 9.372
4. 9.66   **5.** 377.1   **6.** 702.4
7. 24.602   **8.** 2.715   **9.** 34.16
10. 17.29   **11.** 56.886   **12.** 40.15

13. 1.75 meters   **14.** 27.24 kilograms

Page 52: PROBLEM SOLVING: ADDING AND SUBTRACTING DECIMALS

1. 2.66 pounds   **2.** 5.204 quarts
3. 2.8 hours   **4.** 7.44 pounds
5. 0.17 pound   **6.** 4.295 pounds
7. 13.61 pounds   **8.** 1.21 quarts

English Language Arts
Midpoint Review
1. A [RI.5.2]
2A. B [RI.5.1]
2B. *Students should have underlined the sentence:* "Hundreds and hundreds of fireworks have to be made by hand." [RI.5.1]
3. B [RI.5.1]
4A. D [RI.5.4]
4B. *Sample answer:* The root word of "finale" is "final," which means "last." [L.5.4]
5. B [RI.5.6]
6. C [RI.5.8]
7. D [RI.5.2]
8. *Sample answer:* DDT spray hurt the good insects. Birds got sick from eating these insects. The eggs the birds laid had thin shells, which caused them to break before the baby birds were ready to hatch. [RI.5.3]
9A. C [RL.5.4]
9B. *Students should have underlined the word* "squeak." [RL.5.1]
10. D [RL.5.6]
11. B [RL.5.4]
12. *Sample answer:* The main idea is that people blame others instead of taking responsibility. [RL.5.2]
13. *Sample answer:* Both of the boys want to be class president. [RL.5.3]
14. D [RL.5.3]
15. D [RL.5.6]
16. *Sample answer:* Both boys put the same amount of work into their campaigns. They tried different things, but they both worked just as hard. This is why they both won. [RL.5.3]

Writing Midpoint Review
Score students' writing using the rubric on page 164.

Math Midpoint Review
1. 740.08 [5.NBT.3.a]
2. B, C, E
3. ten thousands
   100 times greater [5.NBT.1]
4. $20.61
   $4.39 [5.OA.7]
5. C [5.NBT.6]
6. D [5.NBT.5]
7. 6.543 [5.NBT.7]
8. B
9. A
10. A, C, F [5.NBT.3.b]
11. B [5.NBT.4]
12. 9,372 [5.NBT.5]
13. game 5, game 1, game 3
    game 2, game 4, game 5
14. A [5.NBT.7]
15. A [5.NBT.6]
16. B, D, F [5.NBT.3.b]
17. A, D, E
18. 270 R15 [5.NBT.6]

Week 5
Page 69: SENTENCE FRAGMENTS
Items 1, 3, 4, 5, 6, 9, and 11 should be crossed out because they are fragments. Students should have place periods at the end of the sentences in items 2, 7, 8, 10, 12, 13, 14, and 15.

Page 70: MULTIPLYING AND DIVIDING DECIMALS BY TENS
1. 63.2
2. 8.75
3. 747
4. 36
5. 50.3
6. 6,988
7. 54.9
8. 0.31
9. 190.4
10. 9,700
11. 2,008.6
12. 35,799.2

13. 0.658
14. 0.2784
15. 7.9251
16. 0.0415
17. 3.7157
18. 0.0289
19. 52.96
20. 0.08324
21. 0.153225
22. 9.0525
23. 0.046
24. 0.00178

Page 71: RUN-ON SENTENCES
Students should have circled the letters that are capitalized below and placed punctuation as shown.
1. Pandas like to eat bamboo. It grows in warm areas.
2. Four quarts equal one gallon. What equals a pint?
3. Watch out! There is paint on the floor.
4. Our team is up to bat. What is the score?
5. Do you play a musical instrument? I have always wanted to play the piano.
6. I forgot to have you sign the form. Where did I put it?
7. Can you read that sign from here? What does it say?
8. The bald eagle flies fast. It is a symbol of strength.
9. Jenn chose the paint herself. The room looks very different.
10. The captain spoke to his troops. He ordered them to capture the fort.
11. What a colorful sunset! There's no place like the West.
12. This looks like a good spot for fishing. Let's anchor here.
13. Would you like some peas? May I have the chicken?
14. We went to the concert. The singer was very good.
15. How much do the sodas cost? I would like two.

Page 72: MULTIPLICATION WITH DECIMALS

1. 30.1	**2.** 40.5	**3.** 77.4	**4.** 52.8	**5.** 1,856.4
6. 22.52	**7.** 21.78	**8.** 95.4	**9.** 50.31	**10.** 1,264.95
11. 22.8	**12.** 17.5	**13.** 483.8	**14.** 6.08	**15.** 23.5
16. 1.04	**17.** 28.8	**18.** 1.42	**19.** 8.48	**20.** 94.52

21. 42.5 inches   **22.** 9.45 ounces

Page 73: AVOIDING DOUBLE NEGATIVES

Answers may vary but should be written with only one negative, for example:

1. My mom says I should never leave my clothes on the floor.
2. She can't find any place to walk in my room.
3. Nobody can come into my room until I clean it.
4. I needed clean socks, but I couldn't find any.
5. Soon, I won't have anything clean to wear.
6. I don't have anywhere to put things in my closet.
7. After I'm finished cleaning, you won't find a cleaner room anywhere.

Page 74: DIVISION WITH DECIMALS

1. 8.6	**2.** 9.2	**3.** 0.76	**4.** 0.029
5. 0.96	**6.** 1.7	**7.** 0.056	**8.** 0.009
9. 1.3	**10.** 0.035	**11.** 0.029	**12.** 0.08

13. 2.65 acres   **14.** 0.09 pound   **15.** 0.85 inch

Page 75: SHORT FORMS

Dec., Mr., NC, didn't, ft
weren't, they'd, A., mi, US, Pres.
A. E., hr, min

Page 76: EQUIVALENT FRACTIONS

1. 2	**2.** 2, 2, 6	**3.** 3, 3, 6
4. 4	**5.** 2, 4	**6.** 3, 3, 15

7. 9	**8.** 4	**9.** 12	**10.** 7	**11.** 20
12. 8	**13.** 12	**14.** 5	**15.** 9	**16.** 16

17. 3	**18.** 6	**19.** 8	**20.** 9	**21.** 15
2	$\frac{5}{10}$	$\frac{9}{12}$	$\frac{5}{15}$	$\frac{14}{18}$

22. 12   **23.** 15

Pages 77–78: COMPREHENSION: LITERARY ELEMENTS

1. C
2. A
3. D
4A. B   **4B.** B
5. *Sample answer:* The conflict in the story is between the main character and himself because he cannot say "no" to his friends when they want to play baseball in his backyard. The backyard is the setting and also causes the conflict. The main character has been told to not play baseball in his yard, but he disobeys. This leads to a broken window, which leads to conflict between the main character and his parents.

Page 79: SIMPLIFYING FRACTIONS

1. 8	**2.** 2, 2, 4	**3.** 3, 3, 2
4. 6	**5.** 8	**6.** 6
7. 8	**8.** 6	

9. 4, 4, 2	**10.** 6, 6, 1	**11.** 4, 4, 3
12. 1	**13.** 1	**14.** 4
15. 3	**16.** 1	

17. $\frac{3}{4}$	**18.** $\frac{1}{2}$	**19.** $\frac{2}{3}$	**20.** $\frac{2}{5}$	**21.** $\frac{1}{3}$
22. $\frac{2}{3}$	**23.** $\frac{3}{4}$	**24.** $\frac{3}{5}$	**25.** $\frac{5}{8}$	**26.** $\frac{6}{7}$

27. $\frac{5}{8}$ **28.** $\frac{4}{5}$

Page 80: FRACTIONS AND DECIMALS

Fraction with denominator of 100	$\frac{75}{100}$	$\frac{19}{100}$	$\frac{30}{100}$	$\frac{80}{100}$	$\frac{25}{100}$
Decimal	0.75	0.19	0.3	0.8	0.25

1. $\frac{16}{25}$	**2.** $\frac{9}{10}$	**3.** $\frac{21}{50}$
4. $\frac{19}{50}$	**5.** $\frac{3}{5}$	**6.** $\frac{13}{50}$
7. $\frac{1}{5}$	**8.** $\frac{11}{20}$	**9.** $\frac{9}{50}$

10. $\frac{75}{100}$, 0.75	**11.** $\frac{40}{100}$, 0.4	**12.** $\frac{50}{100}$, 0.5
13. $\frac{25}{100}$, 0.25	**14.** $\frac{70}{100}$, 0.7	**15.** $\frac{60}{100}$, 0.6
16. $\frac{70}{100}$, 0.7	**17.** $\frac{80}{100}$, 0.8	**18.** $\frac{24}{100}$, 0.24

Week 6

Page 81: CONTRACTIONS

1. isn't, don't
2. doesn't, won't
3. Aren't, I'll
4. wasn't, couldn't
5. Don't, They'll
6. haven't, They've
7. Didn't, He's
8. aren't, You're
9. can't, It's
10. We're, I'm

Page 82: ADDING AND SUBTRACTING UNLIKE FRACTIONS

1. 2, 2, 2, 3	**2.** 4, 4, 4, 1	**3.** 3, 3, 6, 1, 7
4. $\frac{11}{12}$	**5.** $\frac{5}{8}$	**6.** $\frac{4}{12}$
7. $\frac{1}{8}$	**8.** $\frac{1}{9}$	**9.** $\frac{4}{15}$

10. $\frac{10}{15} = \frac{2}{3}$	**11.** $\frac{1}{4}$	**12.** $\frac{2}{9}$
13. $\frac{2}{10} = \frac{1}{5}$	**14.** $\frac{15}{18} = \frac{5}{6}$	**15.** $\frac{11}{12}$

Page 83: ISN'T AND AREN'T, WASN'T AND WEREN'T

1. isn't, aren't, aren't, isn't
2. isn't, aren't, weren't, wasn't
3. wasn't, weren't, weren't, wasn't

Page 84: PROBLEM SOLVING: ADDING AND SUBTRACTING UNLIKE FRACTIONS

1. $\frac{1}{2}$ gallon
2. $\frac{7}{8}$ of the turkeys
3. $\frac{1}{4}$ of the cake
4. $\frac{5}{8}$ tank
5. $\frac{4}{15}$ of his pay
6. $\frac{1}{6}$ hour
7. $\frac{3}{4}$ of the pack
8. $\frac{2}{3}$ hour

Page 85: HOMOPHONES

1. rode
2. weak
3. eight
4. new
5. whole
6. pale
7. buy
8. flour

9. write, right
10. way, weigh
11. our, hour

Page 86: MIXED NUMBERS AND IMPROPER FRACTIONS

1. $1\frac{2}{3}$
2. $1\frac{1}{4}$
3. $2\frac{1}{2}$
4. 2, 1, 3
5. 8, 3, 11
6. $\frac{8}{5}$
7. $\frac{25}{9}$
8. 3, 2, 1, $\frac{7}{3}$
9. 2, 2, 1, $\frac{5}{2}$
10. 3, 1, $1\frac{1}{3}$
11. 4, 1, $2\frac{1}{2}$
12. $4\frac{1}{2}$
13. $3\frac{1}{3}$
14. 3, $3\frac{1}{2}$
15. $1\frac{2}{3}$
16. $2\frac{2}{5}$
17. $\frac{10}{3}$ boxes
18. $1\frac{3}{4}$ hours

Page 87: HOMOPHONES

1. there
2. They're, their
3. their
4. They're
5. there
6. their
7. they're
8. there

Page 88: ADDING AND SUBTRACTING MIXED NUMBERS

1. $14\frac{5}{8}$
2. $10\frac{3}{4}$
3. $13\frac{4}{5}$
4. $2\frac{2}{3}$
5. $7\frac{1}{3}$
6. $5\frac{1}{3}$
7. $7\frac{4}{15}$
8. $10\frac{2}{9}$
9. 5

10. $1\frac{11}{12}$
11. $\frac{2}{3}$
12. $4\frac{1}{2}$
13. $\frac{13}{16}$ gallon
14. $7\frac{1}{2}$ hours

Pages 89–90: COMPREHENSION: AUTHOR'S PURPOSE

1. C
2A. D 2B. B
3. C
4. A
5. *Sample answer:* The tone of the passage is casual and lighthearted. The narrator is a young boy who is excited, eager, and helpful to his two aunts. The author's purpose is to entertain with a nice story. He does that by using the lighthearted, upbeat tone to entertain the readers.

Page 91: PROBLEM SOLVING: ADDING AND SUBTRACTING MIXED NUMBERS

1. $2\frac{3}{4}$ pounds
2. $12\frac{1}{3}$ inches
3. $2\frac{5}{6}$ yards
4. $23\frac{3}{10}$ seconds
5. $\frac{5}{6}$ hour
6. $6\frac{1}{6}$ minutes
7. $5\frac{5}{8}$ gallons
8. $3\frac{1}{12}$ yards

Page 92: ADDING AND SUBTRACTING FRACTIONS AND MIXED NUMBERS

1. $\frac{19}{28}$
2. $2\frac{2}{3}$
3. $6\frac{3}{4}$
4. $\frac{7}{8}$
5. $1\frac{1}{4}$
6. $\frac{3}{4}$
7. $7\frac{3}{5}$
8. $\frac{13}{24}$
9. $\frac{1}{2}$
10. $1\frac{1}{8}$
11. $3\frac{1}{10}$
12. $\frac{1}{6}$
13. $\frac{11}{18}$
14. $3\frac{7}{8}$
15. $2\frac{9}{10}$
16. $8\frac{7}{20}$
17. $2\frac{1}{12}$ pounds
18. $39\frac{4}{5}$ pounds

Week 7

Page 93: PREFIXES

1. dis
2. in
3. un
4. im
5. dis
6. in
7. un
8. im
9. dis
10. non
11. im
12. in
13. un
14. non
15. non
16. in
17. un

18. dis

Page 94: MULTIPLICATION AND FRACTIONS

1. 4
2. 3
3. 5
4. 6
5. 2
6. 10
7. 6
8. 8
9. 3
10. $\frac{1}{4}$
11. $\frac{9}{16}$
12. $\frac{7}{32}$
13. $\frac{1}{10}$
14. $\frac{1}{27}$
15. $\frac{4}{7}$
16. $\frac{5}{8}$
17. $\frac{1}{4}$
18. $\frac{1}{4}$
19. 2 gallons
20. $\frac{5}{9}$ quart

Page 95: SUFFIXES

1. prevent
2. act
3. observe
4. invite
5. direct
6. decorate
7. explore
8. locate
9. suggest
10. introduce

11. settlement
12. brightness
13. protection
14. addition
15. imagination
16. confusion
17. improvement
18. strangeness
19. collection
20. admiration

Page 96: MULTIPLYING FRACTIONS AND MIXED NUMBERS

1. $3\frac{1}{2}$
2. $1\frac{1}{9}$
3. $1\frac{3}{4}$
4. 10
5. $16\frac{1}{2}$
6. 22
7. $\frac{34}{35}$
8. $\frac{8}{9}$
9. $4\frac{1}{5}$
10. $\frac{27}{32}$
11. $3\frac{11}{15}$
12. $5\frac{1}{3}$
13. $7\frac{1}{2}$ hours
14. $1\frac{1}{24}$ pints

Page 97: SUFFIXES

ful, ful, less, less, ful, less, ful, ful, ful, less, ful, ful, ful, ful, ful, less

"full of": respectful, playful, powerful, painful, careful, successful
"the amount that fills": roomful, houseful, cupful, mouthful, handful

Page 98: MULTIPLICATION OF MIXED NUMBERS

1. $8\frac{1}{8}$
2. $26\frac{2}{3}$
3. 3
4. $3\frac{3}{10}$
5. $7\frac{1}{2}$
6. $3\frac{3}{4}$
7. $6\frac{3}{4}$
8. 24
9. $11\frac{9}{10}$
10. 8 kilograms
11. $9\frac{5}{8}$ yards

Page 99: PREFIXES AND SUFFIXES

1. preplan
2. repay
3. interstate
4. misuse

5. illness
6. invention
7. measurement
8. arrival

9. discontinue, continue
10. violinist, violin
11. noticeable, notice
12. juicy, juice
13. subplot, plot
14. painless, pain
15. traveler, travel
16. foresee, see
17. unaware, aware
18. childish, child
19. collector, collect
20. disrespectful, respect
21. immovable, move
22. observation, observe

Page 100: PROBLEM SOLVING: MULTIPLICATION OF FRACTIONS

1. $\frac{1}{4}$ pound
2. $43\frac{3}{4}$ hours
3. $\frac{7}{12}$ mile
4. 7 gallons
5. $2\frac{1}{2}$ hours
6. 8 hours
7. $2\frac{7}{10}$ quarts
8. $7\frac{7}{12}$ hours

Pages 101–102: COMPREHENSION: SEQUENCE

1. A
2. A
3A. B
3B. *Students should have underlined the sentence,* "When your wax is very hard, you can take out your candle."
4. B
5. *Sample answer:* The last step is to remove the candle from the mold and take the rock off the top.
6. *Sample answer:* Paragraph 4 tells you how to put the candlewick in the candle. If you forget to do this, the candle will have no wick. Then you will not be able to burn it, so it will not really be a candle at all. It would just be molded wax.

Page 103: DIVIDING WHOLE NUMBERS BY FRACTIONS

1. 4	**2.** 9	**3.** 8
4. 12	**5.** 12	**6.** 8
7. 16	**8.** 5	**9.** 6

10. 12 servings **11.** 24 servings

Page 104: PROBLEM SOLVING: FRACTIONS

1. $1\frac{1}{3}$ feet **2.** $6\frac{2}{3}$ hours

3. 21 points

4. 20 times **5.** 6 times

6. $2\frac{4}{5}$ hours

7. $14\frac{2}{7}$ miles **8.** 28 pounds

Week 8

Page 105: WORD USAGE

learn, a, teach, good, well, an, doesn't, himself
let, leave, sit, lie, who, those, themselves, any, them

Page 106: CUSTOMARY UNITS OF LENGTH

1. 60	**2.** 12
3. 9	**4.** 10,560
5. 4	**6.** 880
7. 80	**8.** 141
9. 37	**10.** 10
11. 2,000	**12.** 5

13. 2, 6
14. 8, 2
15. 1, 4,720

16. 15 feet 6 inches **17.** 6 yards
18. 7 inches **19.** 6 inches

Page 107: COMMA USAGE

1. Hannah, what is Mardi Gras? [b]
2. In New Orleans, Louisiana, it is a holiday. [d, d]
3. This festival, Juan, comes at the end of a long carnival. [b, b]
4. People wear purple, green, and gold. [e, e]
5. There are balls, king cakes, and floats. [e, e]
6. Parades, costumes, and banners were everywhere. [e, e]
7. The first American Mardi Gras was held on March 16, 1766. [c]
8. Well, is it a national holiday? [a]
9. No, it is most famous in Alabama, Florida, and Mississippi. [a, e, e]
10. Actually, Biloxi, Mississippi, and Mobile, Alabama, even have their own Mardi Gras. [a, d, d, d, d]

Page 108: CUSTOMARY UNITS OF CAPACITY AND WEIGHT

1. 2
2. 40
3. 7
4. 8
5. 8
6. 2, 1
7. 10, 5

8. 4
9. $\frac{1}{2}$
10. 1, 6
11. 56
12. 4, 6
13. 9,000
14. 6

15. 3 gallons 1 quart **16.** 27 pounds
17. the 48-ounce box **18.** $2.28

Page 109: DIRECT QUOTATIONS

1. "Didn't he do something with peanuts?" asked Shing.
2. "Yes, he found more than 300 ways to use them," answered Mackenzie.
3. She declared, "Dr. Carver made soap, printer's ink, and even a substitute for milk from peanuts!"
4. Shing added, "He also taught farmers to grow more crops on their land without hurting the soil."
5. "I've chosen Thomas Edison for my report," Joe said.
6. Molly exclaimed, "He's really famous!"
7. "Do you think we'd still be using oil lamps if Edison hadn't invented the light bulb?" asked Mackenzie.
8. Shing said, "I think someone else would probably have invented it."
9. "Well, the person I'm reporting on might not be famous without Edison's help," Molly said.
10. "Who is that?" asked Joe.
11. Molly answered, "I picked Taylor Swift."
12. She continued, "If Edison hadn't invented the phonograph, we might not be able to hear her sing!"

Page 110: METRIC UNITS OF LENGTH

1. 2	**7.** 300
2. 1.5	**8.** 8
3. 650	**9.** 7.25
4. 5,000	**10.** 4.5
5. 168	**11.** 2,500
6. 3,250	**12.** 2.65

13. centimeters
14. kilometers
15. meters
16. meters
17. kilometers
18. centimeters
19. meters

20. 40 bookmarks **21.** 4.8 kilometers

Page 111: DIRECT QUOTATIONS

1. "Do you see that beaver?" asked Brianna.
2. "What strong teeth it has!" exclaimed Kenji.
3. Dion stated, "The teeth are curved for gnawing stumps."
4. Kesha asked, "What is that mound?"
5. "That is the beaver's lodge," explained Eddie.
6. He added, "It's made of chunks of wood."

Page 112: METRIC UNITS OF CAPACITY AND MASS

1.	1 mL	4.	4 L
2.	10 L	5.	100 L
3.	100 mL	6.	6 mL
7.	2,000	10.	5.6
8.	3	11.	9,800
9.	1,500	12.	0.5
13.	1 g	16.	1 mg
14.	1 kg	17.	100 kg
15.	10 kg	18.	25 g
19.	5,000	22.	1,800
20.	7	23.	3,200
21.	1,500	24.	0.7

Pages 113–114: COMPREHENSION: INFERENCES

1. A
2A. B
2B. *Students should have underlined the sentence,* "Since a shark relies on so many senses, when even one sense is not working well, the shark is not able to hunt as well."
3. D
4A. A   4B. C
5. *Sample answer:* The shark would probably first nudge it to see if it is something that it can eat. This would probably show it that the wood is not edible. It may also take a small bite to test it. Then it would also see it cannot eat the wood. So it would swim away and leave it alone.

Page 115: CUSTOMARY MEASUREMENTS

1. $2\frac{1}{4}$ cups
2. 8 ounces
3. 5 pounds
4. 1 pound 2 ounces
5. 3 quarts
6. $1\frac{1}{4}$ pounds
7. 7 ounces
8. $2\frac{1}{2}$ ounces

Page 116: PROBLEM SOLVING: MEASUREMENT

1. 2,640 feet
2. 42 inches
3. 1 meter
4. 1 kilogram
5. $18 less
6. 3 pounds

7. 1.5 liters
8. 1.25 kilometers *or* 1,250 meters *or* 1 kilometer 250 meters

Week 9
Page 117: ALPHABETICAL ORDER

10, 2, 12
6, 8, 1
5, 7, 11
4, 3, 9

1. 5
2. 4
3. 7
4. 1
5. 6
6. 2

Page 118: ORDERED PAIRS

1. (0, 9)
2. (2, 8)
3. (3, 6)
4. (5, 5)
5. (5, 3)
6. (8, 2)
7. (10, 4)

8.	*L*	14.	*G*
9.	*B*	15.	*C*
10.	*H*	16.	*K*
11.	*D*	17.	*I*
12.	*J*	18.	*E*
13.	*A*	19.	*F*

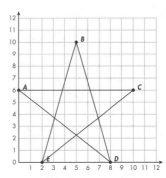

Page 119: HOMOGRAPHS

Answers may vary.
1. something to weigh with
   part of a fish
2. the part of the body that hears
   part of a plant, like corn
3. something to move air with
   an enthusiastic follower
4. part of a fence
   mail
5. a type of bird
6. a fenced-in area for animals

7. to call or signal

8. sliced bread browned on both sides by heat

9. a small building for storage

Page 120: MEASURING ANGLES

1. 90°	**2.** 40°	**3.** 140°
4. 70°	**5.** 90°	**6.** 130°
7. 25°	**8.** 60°	**9.** 110°

Page 121: SYLLABICATION

1. c; hab/it	**2.** a; run/ner	**3.** e; cas/tle
4. a; col/lect	**5.** f; di/al	**6.** b; cer/tain
7. e; cou/ple	**8.** d; bea/ver	**9.** d; cra/yon
10. d; la/bel	**11.** b; tim/ber	**12.** c; lem/on
13. b; mem/ber	**14.** c; fin/ish	**15.** f; ri/ot
16. c; heav/en	**17.** d; crea/ture	**18.** a, e; puz/zle
19. f; re/al	**20.** d; be/yond	**21.** c; cov/er
22. e; tur/tle	**23.** d; ba/con	**24.** b; pic/nic

25. g, i; sun/shine	**26.** g, h; dis/grace
27. i; pan/cake	**28.** h; lone/ly
29. g, i; no/where	**30.** g; or/chard
31. h; pre/fix	**32.** g, h; mouth/ful
33. g, h; speech/less	**34.** i; day/light
35. i; some/how	**36.** i; rail/road
37. h; leaf/y	**38.** g, i; flash/light
39. g, i; eye/brow	**40.** h; re/do
41. g, h; breath/less	**42.** h; un/load
43. g, h; twist/er	**44.** g; bush/el
45. i; wind/shield	**46.** i; school/room
47. g, i; fire/fly	**48.** g, h; mis/spell

Page 122: PERIMETER

1. 15	**2.** 12	**3.** 16
4. 60	**5.** 36	**6.** 48
7. 58	**8.** 100	**9.** 300
10. 12	**11.** 22	**12.** 8

Page 123: DICTIONARY: SCHWA

For items 1–20, the following vowels should be circled:

1. e	**2.** o	**3.** i	**4.** o
5. o	**6.** second e	**7.** u	**8.** u
9. a	**10.** a	**11.** e	**12.** a
13. i	**14.** e	**15.** first e	**16.** i
17. second u	**18.** o	**19.** u	**20.** a

21. d	**31.** n
22. i	**32.** t
23. h	**33.** p
24. c	**34.** s
25. j	**35.** k
26. a	**36.** m
27. f	**37.** q
28. b	**38.** l
29. g	**39.** o
30. e	**40.** r

Page 124: AREA

1. 4	**2.** 45	**3.** 24
4. 400	**5.** 150	**6.** 81
7. 2	**8.** 25	**9.** 20
10. 32	**11.** 50	**12.** 125

Pages 125–126: COMPREHENSION: ANALYZING LANGUAGE

1. D

2. B

3A. B   **3B.** C

4. *Sample answer:* This sentence is an example of foreshadowing. It hints that something amazing is going to happen next. It says that Mary always said something was "Magic." So whatever is going to happen was something Mary will remember and be amazed about in the future.

Page 127: VOLUME

1. 30	**2.** 64	**3.** 20
4. 90	**5.** 280	**6.** 600
7. 105	**8.** 16	**9.** 36
10. 750	**11.** 150	**12.** 72

Page 128: PROBLEM SOLVING: PERIMETER, AREA, AND VOLUME

1. 28 in.	**2.** 15 sq yd
3. 72 cu ft	**4.** 2,808 sq ft
5. 360 ft	**6.** 1,600 cu in.
7. 108 ft	**8.** 720 sq ft

English Language Art End-of-Book Review

1A. A [RL.5.6]   **1B.** A [RL.5.1]

2. B [RL.5.3]

3A. A [RL.5.4]

3B. *Sample answer:* "Sploosh" in paragraph 7 and "shh" in paragraph 15 are both words that help you hear the sound.

4. D [RL.5.6]

5. *Sample answer:* The character in the costume is actually a woman. Sara discovers this when she sees the woman changing into the costume in the restroom.   [RL.5.2]

6. B [RI.5.3]

7. A [RI.5.1]

8. C [RI.5.3]

9. B [RI.5.1]

10. A [RI.5.2]

11. *Sample answer:* The vines must be cut open by other animals.   [RI.5.3]

12. C [RL.5.6]

13A. B [RL.5.4]   **13B.** C [RL.5.1]

14. A [RL.5.4]

15. D [RL.5.4]

16. *Sample answer:* It creates the feeling of a horse galloping.   [RL.5.4]
17. C [RI.5.2]
18. C [RI.5.3]
19. B [RI.5.3]
20. *Sample answer:* The Eiffel Tower was the tallest building in the world and it was made of iron. It became very famous. The Ferris wheel was the tallest ride in the world. It became famous, too.

Writing End-of-Book Review
Score students' writing using the rubric on page 164.

Math End-of-Book Review
1. D
2. $\frac{6}{15}, \frac{13}{15}$ [5.NF.1]
3. $27\frac{1}{24}$ [5.NF.6]
4. C [5.MD.1]
5. 23.707 [5.NBT.7]
6. Point *A:* (−4, 2); Point *B:* (3, 5); Point *C:* (−2, −4); Point *D:* (−3, 1); Point *E:* (0, −2) [5.G.1]
7. B [5.NF.2, 4]
8. 20
   40
9. B, C
10. 4.76 [5.NBT.7]
11. A [5.NF.2]
12. 40 [5.NF.7.c]
13. 2,500
   250,000 [5.MD.1]
14. 9.75 [5.NBT.7]
15. 280
   24 [5.MD.1, 5.b]
16. A, B, D [5.NF.2]
17. 8,000 [5.MD.1]
18. 25
   26.1 [5.NBT.6, 7]

Rubric for Writing Prompts

4	3	2	1	0
The response: Fulfills the requirements of the task	The response: Fulfills the requirements of the task	The response: Fulfills some requirements of the task	The response: Fulfills few requirements of the task	The response is irrelevant, incoherent, incorrect, or illegible.
Uses sentence variety, with some challenging vocabulary	Uses simple sentences with grade-level vocabulary	Uses predominately simple sentences, some sentence fragments, and grade-level vocabulary	Uses sentence fragments or word phrases with below-grade-level vocabulary	
Maintains a clear focus	Maintains a predominately clear focus	Attempts to maintain or establish a clear focus	Does not establish a clear focus	
Is fluent and easy to read and displays a sense of engagement or voice	Is fluent and easy to read and may display a sense of engagement or voice	May be somewhat difficult to read, contains some inaccuracies, and displays no sense of engagement or voice	May be difficult to read, contains many inaccuracies, and displays no sense of engagement or voice	
Uses spelling, grammar, capitalization, and punctuation in a manner that assists considerably in communicating the student's ideas	Uses spelling, grammar, capitalization, and punctuation in a manner that adequately aids in communicating the student's ideas	Uses spelling, grammar, capitalization, and punctuation in a manner that may impede understanding of the student's ideas	Uses spelling, grammar, capitalization, and punctuation in a manner that impedes understanding of the student's ideas	

NOTES

NOTES

NOTES

NOTES